How to Li

When You're a Million Short

"This is a must-have guide that belongs on everyone's bookshelf within easy reach, because in its pages are the answers to how to live like a millionaire without actually being one. It's engaging, funny, and filled with delightful stories and wonderful information on how and where to get the best deals on everything – from Vegas shows to shoes, spas, and adventures at the Spam Museum. Put simply, you will adore Marilyn and her book!" –**Chellie Campbell, Author of** *The Wealthy Spirit* **and** *From Worry to Wealthy*

"*Live like a millionaire . . .* isn't that everyone's dream? Marilyn Anderson understands this dream – and how to achieve it in some very clever, creative ways. Her new book is both inspiring *and* practical – a powerful guide to creating a life you love! –**BJ Gallagher, Author of** *The Power of Positive DOING* **and** *It's Never Too Late to Be What You Might Have Been*"

"*How to Live Like a MILLIONAIRE When You're a Million Short* showed me how I can take women out on amazing dates, spending next to nothing in the process – which is the dream of every red-blooded American male. Thank you, Marilyn Anderson, for enabling my dating life and keeping me from bankruptcy." –**Mark Miller, Blogger,** *Huffington Post* **and Author of** *500 Dates: Dispatches from the Front Lines of the Online Dating Wars*

"Thanks to Marilyn's advice, I enjoyed a six-night stay at a four-star resort in Spain, including accommodations and all meals – for *FREE!* It was an incredible experience." –**Felice Peres, Singer-Songwriter**

"Marilyn Anderson is the master of getting things for free, or at the very least, majorly discounted. I've often grilled her for her secrets. But you don't have to, because she's sharing them with all of us in this book. There's something for everyone, from shopping to dining to theater and beyond. So, listen to her tips, and start saving!" –**Karen Salkin, Social Influencer, and founder/editor/writer of online magazine www.ItsNotAboutMe.TV**

"You're a woman and want to feel like a million dollars – or put a million dollar smile on your face? Read Marilyn's book. And if you're a man, read this little gem of a book . . . you'll put a smile on your woman's face and still be able to put gas in your tank." **–Mark Fisher, Bestselling Author of** *The Instant Millionaire* **and** *The Lazy Millionaire*

"Men, women, college graduates, millennials, baby boomers, or anyone who has felt the sting of the current economy . . . in other words, this book relates to everyone! It's got a ton of information and is beneficial and fun for anyone and everyone who wants to live like a millionaire . . . but just might be a million short." **–Wendy Kram, Producer of** *Mad Money,* **starring Diane Keaton, Queen Latifah, and Katie Holmes**

"For more than a decade, Marilyn Anderson has amazed me with her ability to accomplish the impossible. This book is the recipe for her secret sauce. Don't even hesitate – buy this book and start living like a millionaire!" **– Catherine Clinch, Social Media Strategy Consultant and Writer,** *The Love Boat, Hunter,* **and** *Jake and the Fat Man*

"This is an awesome book with loads of terrific money-saving tips for the good things in life. Marilyn has something for everyone, whether you're a million short or in the chips." **–John Seeley M.A., Bestselling Author of** *Get Unstuck: The Simple Guide to Restart Your Life*

"This book has truly fabulous, amazing and incredible deals!" **–Frank Chindamo, President & Chief Creative Officer,** *Fun Little Movies*

"*How to Live Like a MILLIONAIRE When You're a Million Short* is the smartly-titled new bible for the envious set. No longer shall we live vicariously while others jet-set. Marilyn has opened the gates to divine riches for everyone . . . even those with just a piggy bank. This book pays for itself over and again." **–Joel Eisenberg, author-producer,** *The Chronicles of Ara*

"Reading this book improved my life!" **–Rhonda Miller, Retiree**

"I was struck by Marilyn's book and her web series, *How to Live Like a MILLIONAIRE When You're a Million Short*, not just by how well they are written and produced, which they are, or how funny Marilyn is, which she is – but by how much money she's saving me!" –**Bill Taub, Writer-Producer-Instructor-Author**

"These days, the billionaires are calling the shots. So never tip with anything but green, and read Marilyn Anderson's clever guide a thousand times." – **Gerald Everett Jones, Host of *GetPublished! Radio* and Author of *The Misadventures of Rollo Hemphill***

"As a compulsive bargain hunter, I am impressed with Marilyn Anderson's ability to squeeze every ounce of value out of so many different acquisitions. Now that I have her book I'm giving away my millions." –**Ellis Levinson, *The Consumer Guy***

"Using the tips in this book, I saw three Broadway shows in one week for under $100. Simply amazing. Plus, it's a really fun read!" –**Jennifer Vally, TV Writer-Producer, Comedian**

"How to Live Like a MILLIONAIRE When You're a Million Short captures the essence of the luxury lifestyle and perfectly marries it to the everyday person." –**Michael J. Herman, Author of *Becoming the Complete Champion: One Motivational Minute at a Time***

How to Live Like a MILLIONAIRE

When You're a Million Short

Marilyn Anderson

To Kristin + Ryan -
Enjoy your savings
+
have FUN!
xoxo - Marilyn Anderson

Potpourri Books

Los Angeles, CA

Contents

Introduction

How to Live Like a Millionaire When You're a Million Short?

I've been living that way for the last twenty-five years!

Every year I have my annual 35th birthday party. I always invite a ton of people and, inevitably, the same question always comes up. Everyone wants to know how I live, because they know I have a cool apartment, a hot car, designer clothes, and other expensive things. But what I *never* seem to have is . . . a job. And nobody knows how I do it.

I've taken trips across the country, and to other countries; I've been up in a hot air balloon, and around the course at an auto racetrack; I've sat eighth row center on opening night of a Broadway show, and front row center on closing night of a Michael Feinstein concert.

The strange thing is that many people I know have steady jobs with regular paychecks every month, and they never seem to have any money to do anything. Yet, I often don't get a monthly paycheck – or sometimes *any* paycheck – and still I'm able to enjoy life, even the *high* life, all the time.

One of my screenwriting partners, Ira, told me that all his friends, including some big Hollywood producers, are always asking him, *How does Marilyn live?* Ira said that his friend Ian, who passed away a little while ago, even posed this question at an extremely bizarre time. It seems that on his deathbed, Ian didn't whisper "Tell Mom I love her," or "Say goodbye to my friends," or "I'm sorry I was an asshole." No, with his dying breath, Ian's last words were, *How does Marilyn live?!*

So, in this book, I'm finally going to let the proverbial cat out of the bag and tell people how I do it! Yes, I'm finally going to reveal the secrets of "how I live." I will give all kinds of examples in different categories of how I "live like a millionaire, even though I'm a million short."

I'm going to start by telling you a little bit about my background. And then we'll go into not only how *I* do it, but how *you* can do it, too!

You'll learn all kinds of practical tips for yourself. Oodles of them. But please understand that there's a world of information out there, so I can't tell you "everything." The book would be thousands of pages, and I'd never finish it. And if I did, *you'd* never finish reading it! New opportunities come up every day, and others may disappear. However, you know that old saying: "Give a man a fish, and you feed him for a day. Teach a man to fish, and you feed him for a lifetime." Well, I'm not just going to *give* you fish; I'm also going to *teach* you to fish – that is, for savings and bargains galore – so that, for your lifetime, you too can live like a millionaire, when you're a million short.

Some of the things in this book you'll be able to go out and do tomorrow. Others, you will wish you had done yesterday. Some you may never use; others you may use all the time. Some you may already know; many will be new and enticing. In any case, you will get tons of deals and steals, paybacks, life hacks, and inside tracks! Not to mention, you'll learn a lot about me and how I live like a millionaire when I am *most definitely* a million short.

1. How It All Began

I grew up in a middle-class home in Philadelphia. My parents both worked when I was a child. My dad was an engineer and my mother was a librarian. She arranged the whole house according to the Dewey Decimal System. I was sure that she loved me, because every two weeks she'd renew me! She'd introduce me to her friends as her daughter, Anderson, Marilyn. See "Teenager: geeky, gawky."

Okay, she didn't really say that. But she really was a librarian, and very organized and meticulous in her ways. Both of my parents were extremely organized, ultra-practical, and *uber*-frugal. They were savers, not spenders. Mom and Dad watched their pennies, and taught me to do the same.

Our vacations were nice, but simple. So were our clothes, our home, and our leisure activities. I had a happy and rather normal childhood.

After I got out of college, I found I had become more like my parents. I was, shall we say, frugal. I didn't spend much on clothes, or jewelry, or entertainment, or vacations. I watched my money.

Then, one day, I realized I was being *too* frugal, *too* thrifty. I decided I could still be prudent, but it was time to "spend" on the things I really cared about, while being more economical with things that didn't matter so much to me.

I started spending more on clothes, and loving it. I wouldn't go to an expensive restaurant to eat, because it wasn't important to me.

However, if I saw a dress in a store that I absolutely loved – I would buy it. I would just wait for it to go on sale.

I wouldn't buy an expensive necklace, but I *would* spend money on a play I wanted to see. Only later did I realize that I could see the *same* play, but without spending so much money. And I could eat at that trendy new restaurant *without* paying full price . . . or even anything at all!

When I first got out of college, I had a regular job and a regular paycheck. I had graduated with a Master's Degree in Biology and was working at the National Academy of Sciences in Washington DC running an information service in biomedical research. Actually, I had majored in biology because my mother wanted me to meet a doctor. The trouble was, I met dozens of doctors . . . I just didn't *marry* one!

A few years after working at my science job, I realized it wasn't the right place for me. I was performing in theater on the side, and loving it. In my spare time, I would audition for local plays and dinner theaters and, wonder of wonders – I was getting leads in shows and musicals at local playhouses and dinner theaters. I played Adelaide in *Guys and Dolls*, Ella in *Bells are Ringing*, and Anita in *West Side Story*.

Just picture me, a nice Jewish girl with a Hispanic accent, belting out songs and rolling my R's: *"Puerto Rrrrrrrrrico!" "Trrrropical breezes . . . trrrropic diseases."*

I loved it. The singing, the dancing, and some incredible reviews, such as this one: "Ms. Anderson seems equally accomplished in acting, singing and dancing, and gives a fine, fiery performance."

That was it. I decided I had to do it full time. The truth burst from my soul: I didn't want to be a biologist – I wanted to be a *star!*

So I quit my job, sold my car, sold my furniture, sold my boyfriend (didn't get much for him), and moved to New York to become a star. And guess what! I got into a Broadway show a week after I got to town. Talk about exciting! Wow. I sang, I danced, I acted . . . and I got applause and laughs. And even a paycheck! I was on my way.

Until I got one more thing – a pink slip. Not because "I" wasn't wonderful, but because the production as a whole wasn't very good. Okay, to be honest, it sucked. So, just one week after it opened, it closed. And I was back without a job – or a paycheck – again.

Then I started doing standup comedy for a while. I used to go on back-to-back with another guy who didn't do too well – Jerry Seinfeld! Okay, just kidding, I guess he did pretty well, after all.

That had become my new life. Doing comedy, taking drama classes and singing lessons, and auditioning for acting gigs in plays, commercials and soap operas.

I had been living in Manhattan a couple of years when, one day, I decided I either had to take a vacation or get a job. Let's see, vacation . . . or job? Vacation or *job?* Duh, not much of a contest, huh?

So I took a vacation and went out to Los Angeles. I liked it so much that I never went back to New York.

I had planned to do acting in Hollywood, but I ended up writing instead. I wrote for several different television shows and sold some screenplays for movies.

I was writing a lot of TV and film, and then I wrote my first book, *Never Kiss a Frog: A Girl's Guide to Creatures from the Dating Swamp*. This took me on a whole new journey that was both fun and exciting, because I traveled a lot. I was going all over the country to do book signings and events. But remember, I didn't have a job, and I didn't have an income. (Because books don't usually make an author much money.)

As I was planning my trips, I thought, "Well, as I travel the USA, I can go on my *own* nickel and stay at Motel 6s, or I can go on *somebody else's* nickel and stay at five-star hotels and get *comped* restaurants and *comped* attractions! Which sounds better to you?

I decided I would try to do that . . . by writing travel articles. "Oh no," other *real* travel reporters told me, "You'll never get places to comp you if you don't have an assignment from a big magazine or newspaper. You simply *cannot* do it. The hotels won't do it. No, no, no!"

Hmmm. No? Everyone told me "NO."

Did I listen to them? Uh, NO!

If I had listened, I'd have gone nowhere. Or stayed at every Motel 6 in the country!

But I *didn't* listen. "No" was not a word I understood.

I'm happy to tell you that since then, I've been *all over* this wonderful country of ours. And I've stayed at the most fabulous places. I stayed at a plantation in Natchez, Mississippi; vacationed at the Ernest Hemingway Suite on the top floor of the Hotel Monteleone in New Orleans; was a guest at lodges in St. George, Utah, boutique hotels in New York, resorts in Las Vegas and tons of other four and five-star hotels and inns. I even spent a weekend in the honeymoon suite at the Monterey Beach Hotel and Spa. No, I wasn't married, but I did bring along my lucky boyfriend. Not only did we have two bedrooms, a huge dining room, and a five-course meal at their chic restaurant, but on top of that, midnight champagne and strawberries, breakfast in bed, and a couples massage in their spa. All comped, of course! I also went on an all-expenses-paid, five-star trip to Taiwan for eight days. And you know what? Contrary to what all those "real" travel reporters had told me I'd need – I *didn't* have assignments from a big newspaper or magazine. (And of course, I *didn't* have the big bucks to pay for these awesome places, either.)

What I *did* have was resourcefulness. And what I *did* with it was: I created something for myself. That's what I'm here to tell you and teach you. You can create things for yourself! And no, don't worry – you *don't* have to be a writer.

Obviously, there are a lot of opportunities for writers now, whether you write for a magazine or you create your own blog; however, writing is a definite skill. You might not have writing talent, but you have other talents and skills you may be able to use to help *you* live like a millionaire, when you're a million short.

The sad fact for me was that when you "work" in show business, a lot of the time you are *not* working! Depending on what jobs you get, you might make a lot of money at once; or you might not make any money for a year, or even five years, ten years, whatever. But I always managed to take care of myself and be resourceful, no matter what my income was at any particular time.

Since I left my "real" job as a biologist, my life was to become a series of little jobs, where I would make a chunk of money for a few weeks, and then go back to the ranks of the unemployed for a lonnnnnng time – when no money would be coming in again. It was my lifestyle, and it worked for me.

Through all my different phases, the thing that always used to shock me was that I had friends who had well-paying, full-time jobs, but they *never* seemed to have any money to do things. They always complained of being broke, and never did anything fun.

Meanwhile, I *didn't* have a job, a paycheck, a trust fund, or a husband – yet I was buying clothes, traveling, going to events, living well and enjoying the high life. All my friends wondered "How?" For me, it was just being resourceful and having fun, as well as a few thrilling adventures.

It didn't happen all at once but, over the years, more and more things came my way. And now, I have decided to share it all with you. At first, I taught a course on "How to Find a Bargain." Now keep in mind: a bargain is not something "cheap." I don't like "cheap" things. No, a "bargain" is something fine, something wonderful, or even something expensive – that you get for a really great price. That was how it all started.

But as I've told you, it went much further than that. I like to be generous, not cheap. I like to have fun and adventure. Mostly, I like to *Live Like a Millionaire* . . . even though I have never been close to having a million dollars.

A musical coach I studied with, Albert Hague (who played Mr. Shorofksy on *FAME*), used to tell his students: *Act like you are successful, and people will think you are!* Likewise, I have learned: *Live like a millionaire, and people will treat you like one.* And maybe you even will start to feel like one!

So sit back, relax, and come along with me as I tell you "How to Live Like a Millionaire When You're a Million Short!"

2. That's Entertainment

"Live life fully while you're here. Experience everything. Take care of yourself and your friends. Have fun, be crazy, be weird." –Anthony Robbins

In the current economy, entertainment is one of the things that people consider a luxury. In fact, that's often the *first thing* to go out of their budget. People think, "Oh, we can't spend money on movies; we can't spend money on entertainment, because that is a luxury."

Well, I feel differently. I feel it's important for you to think about what makes you feel good, and *that's* what you *should* spend some of your hard-earned money on. *That's* what makes you *feel rich,* even if you're not! That's right, things that make you feel good aren't a luxury – they're a necessity! Especially in a bad economy when people are depressed or upset or worried, they *need* that release; they need to smile and laugh and be uplifted, and one of the ways you can accomplish this is through entertainment.

As for me, I love laughter, music and socializing, so I go to plays, movies, music clubs and social events every week. If I had to pay full price for all the things I attend, I'd have to BE a millionaire. Since I am not one (yet), I have found a myriad of ways to be able to enjoy all kinds of live theater, concerts, films, theme parks and more for free or really low cost.

The Play's the Thing – Live Theater

I'm a huge fan of live theater, especially musicals. Going to see a musical production with rousing singing and dancing makes me feel exhilarated; it's exciting, fun and enriching. But, it can also be expensive. Extremely expensive! For instance, if you go to New York, Broadway theater tickets can cost over $200 each. Which means, if you're visiting New York and want to go to several shows and have decent seats, you're going to be spending a bundle. But now, I'm going to teach you, you don't have to!

Big Apple Bargains

How YOU Can Enjoy the "Lullaby of Broadway"

> "Broadway has been very good to me. But then, I've been very good to Broadway." –Ethel Merman

New York theaters offer many opportunities for discounts or free tickets. When I visit New York, I love attending the theater. Every night! I'm not kidding. If I go to New York for a week, I'll often go to eight shows! Everyone knows how expensive tickets are there. Can you imagine how much going to eight shows would cost for two people? Well over $1200. But not for me.

Lots of people know about the **TKTS Booth in Times Square** which gives big discounts, and that is definitely an option. However, at the TKTS Booth, you often have to stand in line, sometimes for hours, waiting to buy your discount tickets. As for me, I *love* to get inexpensive seats, but I *hate* to stand in line.

There are many other ways to get discounted tickets. Here are a few I recommend:

A Lottery You Can Actually Win!

Some Broadway shows have what they call a **"lottery."** This is a drawing for theater tickets, where you can win the chance to buy front row or orchestra seats for a tiny fraction of the regular price.

Where and when do these lotteries take place? It used to be that the drawings were held in front of each specific show, and they generally took place two hours before the show started. However, now only a few Broadway shows do in-person lotteries. Most of the shows participate in digital lotteries.

The good news is you don't have to stand and wait at the theater, or even go early. The bad news is that since the lotteries take place online, many more people participate so your odds aren't as good as they were when you had to show up in front of the theater.

Insider Tip

Okay, fans, this is an amazing nugget of info that you may want to keep *all to yourselves.* The fantastic *Hamilton* usually sells tickets for as much as $850 or $1000 per seat. Well, we know *you* can't afford *THAT.* But here's the secret: You can get *first row seats for only $10* through their *online lottery!* (Hey, tell me that little tip isn't worth the price of this book alone!) Whoooopee!!

Each show has specific rules pertaining to when and where you register online to participate in their lottery for that day or evening's performance. You can enter the lottery for as many shows as you like on any day, but if you win, you have a limited time in which to go online and buy your tickets. Each winner is allowed the purchase of two tickets.

Websites for Broadway Ticket Lottery

https://lottery.broadwaydirect.com

www.nytix.com/Links/Broadway/lotteryschedule.html

A few shows still have an in-person lottery, such as *Wicked* and *Book of Mormon.* If the show is at 8 p.m., the lottery takes place at 6 p.m., which means if you get there at ten minutes before 6 p.m., and put your number in the bowl, you'll know, within a few minutes, if you've won. At six o'clock, they draw the lucky numbers. The winners (usually 20 to 30 people) are each allowed to buy two tickets for the show, generally in the *front row,* for anywhere from $20 to $35. And when you take your seats, the people seated right behind you or next to you might have paid $200!

Insider Tip

A secret to doing the live lotteries: if there are two of you going, make a "deal" with two *other* people who are in the lottery. Since each person is allowed to buy two tickets, then if you have four people who have put numbers in, it gives you and your friend an extra chance to get those seats. For instance, you and your friend's name weren't called (boo hoo), but *both* the people you made the deal with got picked, the lucky stiffs! So now, *they* can buy two extra tickets. You each make a deal to sell each other the tickets if your names aren't called, but *both* of their names are.

Depending on the show and the time of year, sometimes there may be 100 people signing up for the lottery, sometimes more. One year, I flew into New York on the

Red Eye, dropped my bags off at my hotel, and headed right over to the noon lottery of the hit Broadway show, *The Book of Mormon*. This fantastic show *had been sold out* ever since it began, and scalpers were getting as much as $800 to $1000 per ticket! When we got to the noon lottery, OMG, the crowd was bigger than any I'd seen before. There were 400 to 500 people standing on the pavement, hoping to win. My boyfriend and I put our names in the bowl (making friends with another couple to increase our chances.) We were prepared to come back other times during the week for the lottery if we didn't win. But Holy Mormony! They called my name fourth, and we got to see *The Book of Mormon* in **front row seats**, for only $32.50 each! It was sooooo exciting!

"I thought it was all a flash in the pan. It wasn't until Broadway came along that I felt I had really made it."
–Julie Andrews

Actually, the whole in-person lottery experience is really fun. Winning makes you feel like a real champion and everyone in the big group is filled with anticipation. The winners usually yell and scream, and it's a hoot. Of course, it's always more fun to win, but some of the people there would come back over and over, since this was such a hot show, and they wanted to see it again and again. Meanwhile, after winning, we even got offered $300 each for our tix, but no way were we selling them! This was the number one show we wanted to see in New York, and it was hilarious. Plus, telling everyone we saw it for only $32.50 in the front row made all our friends at home jealous! Try the lotteries, whether for *The Book of Mormon* or another show. It's fun, and a fabulous way to get discounted seats right in front of others who've paid primo prices.

Hometown Hint: Lotteries Travel with the Show.

Broadway shows that have lotteries usually continue to have them when they go on tour to other cities. So when a Broadway show comes to your neighborhood, call the box office and see if they have a lottery. I saw *Wicked* in Los Angeles, seated in the first row, because I won the lottery. It was sensational and oh-so-much-more-fun because I won!

Some shows that have lotteries are *The Book of Mormon, Kinky Boots, Fun Home, The Lion King, On Your Feet, Aladdin, An American in Paris, Cats,* and *Matilda.*

Push Your Tush and Rush for Rush Seats!

Rush Seats are often more common than the lotteries. Broadway theaters, Los Angeles theaters, and venues in other cities sometimes offer what they call a General or Student Rush. For Student Rush seats, you'll need proof that you attend a school or university. General Rush tickets are available to everyone.

In New York, many Broadway theaters offer Rush Tickets. In Los Angeles, they often have general rush seats available at the Geffen Playhouse and at the Pantages. These are tickets that are offered the same night that you're planning to go to the theater. They are generally "first come, first served."

Depending on the theater, they can be offered first thing in the morning when the box office opens, or sometimes it's right before the show begins. If the performance isn't full, the theater will open up the rush seats and you can buy a ticket. They might cost from $20 to $40 depending on the theater and production. And, again, people who spent $100 or $200 for a ticket might be seated right next to you! Check the theater and productions in your area to see if they offer Rush Seats.

Websites for New York Rush Seats:

www.show-score.com/discounts

www.BroadwayforBrokePeople.com

www.nytix.com/Links/Broadway/lotteryschedule.html

You can find the theaters offering both Rush Seats and Lottery Seats on their schedules. The show-score.com site even offers free tickets to people who review six or more shows.

> "Initially, I wanted to be an ice skater, but then when I was 13 I saw *Bye Bye Birdie*, and that was it – I wanted to be on Broadway." –Liza Minnelli

Other NYC Theater Discount Offers

If you're going to go to New York, and you're not sure you want to do the rush seats or the lottery and you don't want to stand in line, there are a number of websites where you can get other kinds of discount tickets. Sometimes they'll give you a code that you can use, either to order tickets online or to redeem right at the box office of the show you want to see.

Some Sites for New York Show Discounts:

www.TheaterMania.com

www.Playbill.com

www.BroadwayBox.com

www.todaytix.com

By ordering tickets on these sites, you don't have to wait in line, and you don't have to worry if you're going to be lucky and win the lottery or not. You go online and buy them, or you get coupons or codes and go directly to the box office of the show and get a reduced price right there. The TheaterMania and Playbill websites also have lots of cool articles and information about theater.

Todaytix also has an **app** that lets you enter ticket lotteries, buy Rush tickets, set show alerts and more. This app is available in other cities, too, including Boston, Chicago, Connecticut, Los Angeles, Philadelphia, Seattle, San Francisco, Washington DC, and London.

Waaaaay Off Broadway

"I really cut my teeth on off-off-off Broadway shows."
–Bea Arthur

In Los Angeles, if you go to the Ahmanson Theatre, tickets can cost as much as $150 each. But did you know that you can go the Ahmanson on opening night and sit in that $150 seat for *free?* It sounds crazy, but it's true.

"How?" you ask. Well, I'm going to tell you! Every *opening night* at the Ahmanson and every opening night at the Mark Taper Forum and the Kirk Douglas Theatre, the producers give out a lot of tickets to the press and VIPs, and you know what? Because these are free tickets, many times the recipients don't show up.

The theater doesn't want these seats to be empty because they want to: A) support the cast; B) make the press feel like it's a big house; C) get a good audience response, whether it be big laughs or lots of applause.

So the theater has a standby line, which means that every opening night, probably at least 50 to 100 people from the standby line will get in . . . *for free.* Does it mean you sit in the rafters? Not necessarily. If someone in the orchestra seat, eighth-row-center, doesn't show up, guess what! *YOU* get that seat, an eighth-row-center seat . . . and *you* get to see the show for *FREE.* Of course, these theaters are in Los Angeles, but you can check with the theaters in your city to see if they have similar policies. Call their audience services department and ASK!

Have a Cool Night with Hot Tix

The Ahmanson, Mark Taper Forum, and Kirk Douglas theatres in Los Angeles all offer **Hot Tix,** which are nice because you don't have to wait until the night of the show to know if you'll be able to get in. You can usually buy Hot Tix right when the show opens *for any date that you want,* and again it's a low-cost ticket. It's generally $20 or $25. Sometimes they're in the mezzanine or balcony, so the seats might not be as good as Rush Seats or Lottery Tix. But again, it's a very discounted price for a show that would normally cost a whole lot more. Check the theaters in your city to see if they have Hot Tix.

> **"The theater is so endlessly fascinating because it's so accidental. It's so much like life." –Arthur Miller**

Discount Theater Groups

Available in many cities, **www.Goldstar.com** is a website that offers discount tickets to theater and concert venues as well as other entertainment events, all at reduced prices. Signing up with Goldstar is free; you only pay when you order tickets. The tickets are discounted, and there is a small service fee. Another site to get half-price tix (or sometimes free tix) in Los Angeles is **www.Plays411.net.** It's free to sign up, and you can get on their mailing list, or check their website for what's playing when and for how much.

The Los Angeles discount theater groups that I prefer are **www.TheaterExtras.com** and **www.SoldOutCrowd.com.** As a member of these, you join for a nominal annual fee, and you receive free tickets to events and shows ALL YEAR LONG, paying only a $4.00 service fee for each ticket at Sold Out Crowd, or $4.50 at Theater Extras, which also has New York and Las Vegas sites. You can become a member of Sold Out Crowd for $65 or a Gold member for $95. I recommend the Gold Membership as you often get better shows, or get them first.

Insider Tip

If you join **Sold Out Crowd** and mention my name, *Marilyn Anderson*, as the person who referred you, you will get your first four tickets absolutely free, with no service charge! That means a $16 credit towards your service fees.

With SoldOutCrowd.com and TheaterExtras.com, with just the annual fee, you can go to theaters, large and small, almost every night of the week and take a friend, since every membership allows you to order two tickets to every show. I'm not allowed to mention the venues, but I'll tell you they are sometimes the biggest theater venues in Los Angeles, with shows that are on their way to Broadway, or on the first stop on their tour after Broadway.

I love SoldOutCrowd.com and use it all the time. It's a great way to take a friend or date out to a show; they'll be oh-so-impressed, and they don't have to know that you got your tickets for free. They'll probably take you to dinner first, too!

www.Fillaseat.com is a similar annual fee membership website that offers free tickets in the Los Angeles area as well as in Las Vegas, Phoenix, San Diego, Dallas, Houston and San Antonio. Check their site to find out the annual fee and offers in these cities.

It's a Bird . . . It's a Plane . . . It's the Entertainment Book!

The Entertainment Book not only offers discounts on theater tickets (generally, "buy one, get one free"), it offers thousands of discounts on all kinds of things, including theme parks, museums, aquariums, restaurants, hotels, car rentals, retail stores, etc. The book is often available through charities, sometimes at bookstores or car washes, or you can buy it online at **www.entertainment.com**. They have editions for cities all over the United States and Canada.

Other Entertainment Discounts

Sometimes, I've seen stores at malls indicate that if you spend a certain amount on a given day, they'll give you two free tickets to a

Broadway show or concert, touring in your city. At other times, you may find flyers with discount codes at various shops in your city.

Wanna Score Big?

www.Scorebig.com is another site offering discounts in lots of cities, on shows, concerts and sporting events, too. Although I haven't yet used it, I get offers from them, including additional bonus discounts for certain events. This site seems to be almost like a Priceline kind of set up for shows and events, meaning they tell you what regular seats cost, and you can make a bid, telling them what you're willing to pay for tickets, and they either accept it or don't. Since I haven't tried it yet, I can't judge how it works, but they often have big concerts and sporting events that the other groups don't offer.

> "You know what's a great way of tricking people into thinking you're a genius? Write a show about geniuses!" –Lin-Manuel Miranda

Pay What You Can

What does that mean? Exactly what it sounds like. PAY . . . WHAT YOU CAN or What you WANT, or What you can AFFORD! Many theaters across the country have Pay-What-You-Can nights. Los Angeles, Washington DC, New York, Chicago, Atlanta, even London when you go there for a trip.

One of my favorite small theaters in LA is The Actor's Gang, run by the Hollywood star, Tim Robbins. I saw *Lysistrata* at The Actor's Gang. Tickets are regularly $40 each. And I invited a friend, so that would be $80. Eeeek. That's an expensive evening for me. But here's the ticket . . . or *my* ticket. Every Thursday night the theater has a Pay-What-You-Can Night. Which means, instead of $40 or $80, you can pay $10 or $5 or even ONE DOLLAR. It's up to you and what you can afford. As you walk in they have a bowl; you put in your donation (you don't have to "show" anyone how much), and they give you a ticket.

This is for ALL their shows every Thurs night. Btw, the show at The Actors' Gang was hilarious, and I even got to say hi to Tim Robbins in the lobby!

Check your city to see which theaters there have Pay-What-You-Can nights.

You Don't Have to Sing to Be an "Usher"

I'm not talking about the singer, songwriter, dancer and actor, Usher. Although you might be able to see him for free by doing this! Every theater needs ushers. Sometimes these are paid positions, but oftentimes, theaters will use volunteers. Ushers get to see the performances for free, whether it's the actual show they are ushering for, or possibly another one at that venue on a day they aren't volunteering. In Los Angeles, the Geffen Playhouse always looks for ushers. It's great for retired folks on a fixed income who love the theater but don't want to pay high prices.

Ushering is also a great choice for students or young people who want to break into theater. Not only does it look good on their resumes when they say they worked for a theater, it's also a way for them to meet some of the producers, directors or actors who can help them later in their career. I have several friends who have ushered at the Geffen Playhouse in Los Angeles, and I know a young lady who ushered at the Wadsworth Theatre during her senior year. She loved it, and she even got paid as an usher there! In fact, the Geffen also now pays their ushers $10/hr.

http://www.geffenplayhouse.org/usher.php

A retired friend of mine, living in Austin, Texas, is a volunteer usher for the Long Center, a prestigious venue that gets many excellent concerts, operas, plays and events. And the best part, of course, is that you get to see the shows, but you don't have to pay the hefty prices.

Dress Rehearsals and Previews

Preview tickets to shows are often much less expensive than after the show has officially opened, especially if it gets good reviews. Some theaters or productions allow people to attend dress rehearsals free of charge in order to see the audience response. A few decades ago, I was walking around Times Square when some young actors were giving away free tickets to a brand new musical, previewing at the Joe Papp Theater. They wanted to gather an audience for the show. No tickets had been sold, since no one had ever heard of it. I graciously took the complimentary ticket and hopped a short subway ride for a fourth row center seat for the debut of a new musical: *A Chorus Line*!

We all know what happened with that show; it became a humongous hit that went on to win tons of awards, including nine Tony Awards and a Pulitzer Prize, before becoming a movie. And I saw it during its initial performances . . . for *FREE!*

> "Actors are agents of change. A film, a piece of theater, a piece of music, or a book can make a difference. It can change the world." –Alan Rickman

Now please, remember, if you ARE a millionaire – or even if you're not, but can afford it – please support your local theaters by buying seats at regular prices. Otherwise, you can PAY WHAT YOU CAN, join the LOTTERY, get RUSH TIX or HOT TIX, find online discount sites, join SoldOutCrowd.com, or USHER for a night of great enjoyment.

Sin City Savings on Shows

What Happens in Vegas Stays in Vegas . . . but not these money-saving secrets!

I'm not a gambler, but I love Las Vegas. There's simply nowhere else on earth where you have such a selection of entertainment choices. They've got headlining singers and comics, Cirque du Soleil shows, and splendiferous variety shows. You can see ventriloquists and hypnotists, female impersonators and male prestidigitators. Not to mention underwater dancers and boob extravaganzas! Between the shows and restaurants, you could spend a fortune in a week and not have put down one poker chip or pulled the handle on one slot machine.

But take heart; to see the shows, you don't have to spend a fortune, and certainly not full price for anything. There are **half-price ticket booths** at numerous locations along the Strip to get tickets for shows that night as well as discounts at all kinds of restaurants. Find the locations and info at **www.tix4tonight.com**.

There are also many online sites that offer discounted Vegas shows if you want to purchase them in advance before you go there. Some of these include:

www.Vegas.com/deals

www.BestofVegas.com/Las-Vegas-Deals

www.SmarterVegas.com

DO YOUR RESEARCH and you can go to Sin City and not have to spend a lot of money. Just don't lose it at the tables or in the slots. Better still, WIN!

And don't forget, part of the very best entertainment in Las Vegas is just walking through the many decadent hotels on the Strip. You don't have to stay at the trendiest hotels to stroll alongside the millionaires who vacation in their penthouses. Walk through the sumptuous lobbies, look at the amazing architecture, opulent interiors and unique features, and window shop their lavish stores. It's all fun and free! Put on your walking shoes and visit The Venetian, The Bellagio, The Palazzo, Mandarin Oriental, Caesar's Palace, and Aria. Also, if you have kids, Circus Circus is a must.

"Everything and anything you want to do, you can do in Las Vegas." –Drew Carey

Let's Go to the Movies!

Maybe your grandparents or great grandparents remember when they could go to the movies for twenty-five cents. And popcorn was only a nickel. Those times are long gone. In a lot of cities, even the so-called bargain matinee is gone. Nothing seems like a bargain anymore. In Los Angeles, movie prices have gone wild. An adult ticket to a theater can cost anywhere from $13 to $20. And popcorn and a drink: $200! Okay, just kidding, but you know it's a lot.

So who wants to go to the movies at those prices? You figure you'll just stay home and watch it when it comes to Netflix. I prefer to see movies on the big screen. The *really* big screen. I like the experience of sitting in a dark theater with a whole audience, laughing, or getting scared, or just enjoying my two hours without background distractions that I always have at home. But I NEVER pay the full prices at a movie theater.

Living in Los Angeles, we're especially lucky because we get a lot of marvelous movie-going events that other cities might not have. But the truth is, lots of other cities have opportunities also.

Film Festivals Fun

One example is Film Festivals. In Los Angeles, when the American Film Institute (AFI) Film Festival is there, if you sign up to volunteer, you can go to all of their screenings for free.

Many other cities have Film Festivals, too, so check online, in your local newspaper, or at your local Chamber of Commerce to see what's going on in your city for which you can volunteer and get some free tickets or other cool perks.

> "Life moves pretty fast. If you don't stop and look around once in a while, you could miss it." –Ferris Bueller's Day Off

There are a lot of different groups available that offer people free movie screenings near where you live. Whether it's a movie studio, a meetup group, or a film appreciation class, movies are terrific for an evening out or a weekend afternoon. There are often focus groups that want to see how audiences react, and these companies give away tickets for screenings. Sometimes you may have to wait in line, but take a friend, have some fun, and see a free movie.

In addition, you can check with colleges or universities that have Adult Education or Extension classes. They frequently offer film appreciation classes where you pay a nominal fee for the year to see films every week. Oftentimes, cast or crew from the film will appear in person for a panel discussion after the film presentation. A friend of mine took a class at UCLA which cost about $180. For that price, he got to see about 100 movies during the year, and take a friend, too. Not to mention, meet other people with similar interests.

Another membership organization for film enthusiasts in LA is **www.SaturnAwards.net**. You join with an annual membership and get to see about 100 new films on weekend mornings. A regular membership for $195 allows you two seats to every weekend screening. A premium membership for $245 includes all the benefits of a regular membership and also allows you to attend other special events, plays and screenings during the week.

And the Academy Award Goes To . . .

In Los Angeles, there are additional opportunities to see free films, especially around Oscar time. The Wrap is an entertainment and media news website where you can sign up for their Awards and Foreign Screening Series to see free films and lots of Q&A panels with the actors, writers or producers. You may have to be in the film industry (or say you are), or if you live in LA, you probably know someone who is. They offer tons of free screenings which are always fun to attend. Just going to their website at **www.thewrap.com** you can view short films that are up for awards, plus there are all kinds of interesting articles about the biz.

The Los Angeles Times sponsors The Envelope Screening Series which offers free tickets to movies that have Q&A's afterwards, and you often even get free popcorn and soda, too! Additionally, they have evenings featuring discussions with the creators and producers of popular television shows. You don't have to be in the Entertainment Industry to sign up to get two tix for each of their events. Guild Members get preference, so you might have to get there early and wait in line to be guaranteed a seat. Events are held at a theater in Sherman Oaks.

www.events.latimes.com/envelope

Also during the Awards Season, people who love documentaries can be treated to The IDA Documentary Screening Series that offers some of the year's best documentary films at The Landmark Theater in Los Angeles. Screenings conclude with a moderated Q&A with the filmmakers and there are often receptions as well. You can get information and sign up for their screenings at:

http://www.documentary.org/screenings

Viva La France!

Another opportunity for free movies in Los Angeles is the **COLCOA French Film Festival.** This is a nine-day-long festival of French films, held every April at the Director's Guild on Sunset Boulevard. Some of the films, mostly premieres, have a nominal cost, but many of them are free. Every morning there is a free movie. (It's the film that got the most positive reactions among the screenings the day before.) Not only is the movie free, but a there's also a free continental breakfast for those who attend. And at the end of the Festival, one lucky attendee gets a free trip to Paris!

Insider Tip

All the COLCOA movies are free for members of the Writers Guild of America (WGA) and Directors Guild of America (DGA), and they are allowed two tickets each, so if you're not a member, call one and tell them about this, making sure they'll take you as a guest!

The COLCOA French Film Festival also has free panels with the French filmmakers after many of the screenings and free receptions with wine and cheese throughout the week. Check out their website at:

www.Colcoa.org

Free Screenings All Year

Speaking of Guild Members, if you know any actors, writers, directors or people in the biz – the professional entertainment unions SAG, WGA, DGA, and TV Academy offer their members *free screenings all year long,* and they can bring a guest. So what are you waiting for? Get out there and make some new friends!

It Pays to Join If You Don't Have to Pay!

Another screening series in Los Angeles offering free movie screenings followed by Q&A panels with the filmmakers is run by Jeff Goldsmith at Unlikely Films. He sends out an email invitation for different movies; you can sign up and bring a guest. Respond immediately and get to the screenings early, as there is often a line. You can sign up for the email list and get more information at

http://www.unlikely.com/screenings.html

Don't *Discount* Discount Tickets

If you can't go to any of the special screenings, there are other ways to get movie discounts. The first matinee of the day is often cheaper than later shows, and at some theaters, it's all matinees before 6 p.m. Stores such as Costco sell packs of discounted tickets for various movie chains, as does the Entertainment Coupon book. Discounted movie tickets are also sometimes available through various charities, organizations, or your workplace. Some banks and phone companies offer them, too. Of course, most theaters offer lower-cost Student Prices or Senior Prices, and some venues have certain days of the week when tickets are cheaper. In addition, if you sign up for their email or apps, many theater chains will send you special offers and coupons, and some even have Sneak Preview clubs where they invite you to attend selected screenings for free. Check with the theaters near you and "ask" about their discount programs.

Comedy, Music, and More

If you love comedy, many clubs have open-mike nights that are free and frequently music venues have them, too. In addition, many nightspots have different bands on various nights that have no cover, including hotel lounges near you that may offer jazz, blues or pop for the price of a drink, or even for just sitting around to enjoy the vibes.

What's a Bargain? vs. What a Bargain!

This makes me go back to the idea of a bargain. To me, a bargain is not something that's cheap; a bargain is something that you really want, which you get at a good price. It's not something cheap, because I don't like cheap things. I like things that I *want to do* that

I can *get for less,* and that's the kind of information I like to share with you.

> **"Life is like a box of chocolates. You never know what you're gonna get."** –Forrest Gump

Live Television Events and Tapings

If you live in Los Angeles or New York, or are visiting, there are wonderful ways to enjoy live events with celebrities. Go to a television taping. Talk shows like *Ellen, Jimmy Kimmel, The View, The Talk, Live with Kelly,* and *Dr. Phil* all have live studio audiences. Not only do you get to enjoy the show, but there are often giveaways. Remember how Oprah even gave away CARS! Unfortunately, Oprah doesn't have her show anymore, and audiences aren't getting cars (although I did recently see Jimmy Kimmel give away a brand-new Volvo to a woman at a car wash), but TV shows do frequently give gifts to their audiences. You can get hundreds of dollars-worth of gifts just for attending.

I went to a taping of a pilot for a new show, where they gave out VIP seats for another show, *Dancing with the Stars.* On some of the shows, you may be filmed in the audience, and get to see yourself when it airs. Between takes, they usually have a comic doing bits or asking questions, or even letting you dance on the floor during a break in the taping. Plus, you get to see stars in person, along with behind-the-scenes outtakes, etc.

A great time to get tickets to live talk shows is during the weeks before Christmas, since the gifts to audiences at holiday time tend to be really special and often expensive. Ellen is known to be generous to her guests all the time, but if you're lucky enough to score tickets to her show the month before Christmas, you'll be well rewarded and very excited. She has become the new Oprah when it comes to holiday gifting!

During the holidays, many shows have segments showing cool gift ideas. And guess what! The audience members get to take home all the products shown on the air. Hey, what are you doing next Christmas? Let's go!

Tickets for many television shows can be attained through:

> www.audiencesunlimited.com
>
> www.on-camera-audiences.com
>
> www.onsetproductions.com
>
> www.tvtix.com

For some television shows, you go to the ticket booth where they are filmed, whether it be Paramount Studios, NBC, ABC or CBS.

By the way, these shows are not necessarily only in LA and New York. Jimmy Kimmel did a week of shows in Austin, while Pat Sayjak takes *Wheel of Fortune* on the road to many different cities. Then there are shows that film in Nashville, Vancouver, and other places, too.

In addition to talk shows, some television comedies have live audiences. So you can go and see the actors live and in person as they tape the show.

And the Winner Is . . . YOU!

Don't forget there are TV shows that give you a chance to *win* cash and prizes, too. They call them **game shows!** Do a search online to find out which ones are looking for contestants. If you are feeling smart, *Jeopardy* actually goes around the country to interview potential contestants. Who knows, you might make a million the easy way!

Years ago, I was on several game shows, including *The $10,000 Pyramid* and *Sale of the Century*, where I won a portable dishwasher and then sold it. On Pyramid, I won $40 and a set of Lego Building Blocks. I don't have any kids, so I sold them, too. Even though I didn't win big, they were both experiences I'll always remember.

For most game shows, studio audience tickets are available directly by phone, mail, or through their official website. Check out the shows you like and order free tickets. Some sites advertising for contestants include:

> http://www.starnow.com/casting-calls/tv-reality/game-shows/
>
> https://www.castingcallhub.com/tryout/game-show/
>
> http://gameshows.about.com/od/beacontestant/a/casting_calls.htm

Sometimes, shows even *pay* audience members to show up! This happens often with new shows where people don't know about them yet. Once in a while, Craigslist has listings for them under Jobs: TV/film/video, part-time, et cetera, or miscellaneous. Another way to see stars and VIPs is to volunteer at your local PBS station to answer phones during their membership drives. This gives you the opportunity to meet famous people and get deals on the promotions from their station. It's entertaining and fun as well as *free*!

Take Your Seats, Everyone!

If you love to get up close and personal with stars, whether they are actors, musicians or celebrities, you can stalk one and maybe get arrested, or you can become a **Seat Filler.**

They have seat fillers for the Academy Awards, the Emmys, the Grammys, People's Choice Awards, SAG Awards, Country Music Awards, and American Music Awards, to name just a few.

What's a Seat Filler?

Just what it sounds like. You fill the seat of someone when they get up and leave it for a while. When award shows are filmed, cameras frequently pan the audience, and the last thing the producers want is for the auditorium to look empty. So when the celebrities get up to accept their award (or if they need to go to the bathroom, or to a corner to cry over their loss, or outside to calm their nerves with a cigarette or a drink or a snort), there are going to be a lot of empty seats in the room. That's when they need regular people to look like they belong there and fill in! You'll need to dress formal, but don't worry. You can rent a stunning outfit, including jewelry, to look the part, as I explain in the chapter on "So You Think You Can SHOP!"

Being a seat filler is a ton of fun and an experience you'll always remember. Just telling your friends you're going to the Academy Awards or the Grammys will make them envy you. And sometimes, you are even on camera. You'll be sitting with millionaires, and looking like one, too. You can schmooze with them and, who knows, you may even get invited to an after-party!

Some sites to get info and sign up are:

www.seatfillersandmore.com

www.tvtickets.com/seatfillers.htm.

Dating, Mating, or Single . . . Enjoy a Tight Night Out!

It's Friday night. You'd love to go out. But you're kind of broke! You can go have a cup of coffee at Starbucks. Or would you rather have a night with wine, food and culture . . . for *zero*?

I meet a lot of men through Internet dating. And on a first date, so many guys invite a girl for coffee. Because it's cheap, and so are they! But guys, you can do better than that, and not have to spend anything! So don't invite her for coffee. PLEASE!

Or maybe you're a couple who's strapped for dough. Are you going to go to Starbucks? No way! That won't impress a new girl *or* one you've known for years. Sitting in a room with a bunch of people staring at their laptops? Not my idea of romance . . . or any night out! I'm going to tell you how you can have an amazing evening with wine, hors d'oeuvres and hobnobbing with the wealthy . . . and not spend a penny! OMG, how to do it?

Go to an Art Opening

Especially on Thursday, Friday or Saturday nights, lots of galleries have openings. They're generally open to the public, and guess what! They serve wine, and sometimes food, and you can see fabulous art . . . as well as doing some serious, fun people-watching.

A couple of weeks ago, I went to a gallery in Santa Monica. I was looking at a painting, and asked how much it was. The clerk said, "Three-fifty." Hmmm, I thought, three hundred fifty dollars, that's reasonable. Except, it wasn't $350 . . . *it was $350,000!* And the man next to me bought it!

Let me tell you, it was an awesome evening with wine, appetizers, and more than a few millionaires. Another time I was at an opening in Santa Monica, and the first people I saw were Kim Kardashian and Kanye West. Then I saw Goldie Hawn and Kurt Russell. Then, on the other side of the room, looking at a painting, was Barbra Streisand!

Fun Tidbit

I had actually met Barbra's husband, James Brolin, at an event (which I went to for free, of course) about a year before he met Barbra. James was charming and friendly and we had a great conversation. Cut to: this art event many years later, where I saw him standing by himself. Remembering how nice James had been to me, I started to walk over to him. I planned to say, "I met you a long time ago, and I realize you married Barbra because she reminded you of ME!" It would have been fun to see his reaction.

However, just as I was walking over, Barbra appeared by his side and lovingly grabbed his arm. Oops, that stopped me in my tracks. I certainly couldn't say it to him while she was there, and I was too shy (believe it or not) to say hello to Barbra herself. But I thought, how cool would it have been to reconnect with James Brolin and have a laugh. Or have him look at me like I was a totally crazed lunatic!

Now I'm not saying you'll necessarily see celebs when you go to art openings in your area, but you will see lots of interesting people.

So How Do You Find the Art Openings at Galleries?

Check the local papers, or go online for events taking place in your city. Here in Los Angeles, the *LA Weekly* lists all the openings. Also, there are specific areas in each city that have lots of galleries in one place. Here, it's Bergamot Station in Santa Monica, and on Melrose Avenue, La Brea Avenue, and certain streets in Beverly Hills or Downtown Los Angeles.

> **"The purpose of art is washing the dust of daily life off our souls."** –Pablo Picasso

You can go into a gallery any day and put your name on their mailing list, and you'll start getting invited to their openings.

It's a great way to spend an evening *without* spending any money; you'll be mixing with millionaires and having a blast. And hey, if you're not taking a date, maybe you could even *meet a millionaire* there! Be sure to dress to impress, too, which at an art gallery could mean anything from a little black dress to a funky artsy outfit. You'll see people wearing all kinds of chic, trendy apparel or crazy, wacky clothes, and that's part of the fun.

Lots of neighborhoods have many galleries in one area or on a particular street where they have special nights or days when they are all open for festivities. Check in your city or in places a short drive away. Laguna Beach has an Art Walk the first Thursday of the month, and art festivals all summer long. Different areas of LA feature many Art Walks at different times of the year that are super fun; you stroll from place to place, viewing the art, drinking wine, and meeting friendly people. In Santa Fe, New Mexico, a Christmas Eve tradition is to parade the Canyon Road Farolito Walk alit with lanterns and luminarias that line the promenade famous for its art galleries.

Speaking of Art – Museum Musings

> "I went to a museum that had all the heads and arms from all the other museums." –Steven Wright

I love museums. You can spend days at a time wandering through them, looking at wondrous art and learning about history. You're surrounded by incredible, expensive and irreplaceable treasures that give humanity a reflection of itself and a reminder of the beauty created through the ages. Also, they are great places to meet people.

No matter what your interest, there's a museum for you. There are art museums, natural history museums, car museums, flying museums and any kind that you can think of, even erotica museums. If enough people are interested in something, there's probably a museum for it somewhere.

When I was traveling through Minnesota, I went to the Spam Museum. Not the spam in emails, but the Spam you eat. This was a fabulous, fun and innovative museum, where they had a movie by Al Franken, and a section where you could even practice packaging Spam yourself! I was like the Lucille Ball of canning Spam. And I even came home with Spam earrings! Although the museum closed at the end of September, 2014, it had a "grand can reopening" in April, 2016, in Austin, Minnesota.

"The aim of art is to represent not the outward appearance of things, but their inward significance." – Aristotle

Depending on the museum, admissions can be anywhere from free to a significant amount, especially if you're taking a whole family. But even at places where they charge considerable entrance fees, there are usually ways and days to get in free. Many places have a free museum day, when the visitors don't pay regular prices.

For example, at the Los Angeles County Museum of Art, it's free the second Tuesday of every month; the Norton Simon Museum is free the first Friday of every month from 5 to 8 p.m., and the Autry National Center of the American West is free the second Tuesday of every month. Check for your city's museums at:

www.freeMuseumday.org

If you have a Bank of America credit card, they offer their customers free admission to 150 museums around the country and other discounts, too. Check with your bank to see what they offer.

http://promotions.bankofamerica.com/deals/

A **nationwide free museum** day takes place on a Saturday in September, when more than 1,400 museums across the country waive admission for the annual Museum Day Live! hosted by Smithsonian Magazine.

www.smithsonianmag.com/museumday

Some of the most popular museums participating in the event include:

CHICAGO: Loyola University Museum of Art

LOS ANGELES: GRAMMY Museum

NEW YORK: Mount Vernon Hotel Museum & Garden

SAN FRANCISCO: Bay Area Discovery Museum

WASHINGTON DC: Smithsonian's National Air and Space Museum

AARP and AAA offer their members lots of discounts on various activities and events; sometimes there's a code to use, other times you just show your card to get a discount. This can work at museums, theaters, attractions, and restaurants, too.

Also, check the Human Resource department at the company where you work. Businesses often have discount coupons for all sorts of things. You can check by simply asking – or if they have a company newsletter, discount offers will frequently be listed there.

When you travel, remember that tourist offices, chambers of commerce, and hotels have coupons or discount offers for various entertainment venues, like shows, theme parks and attractions in the area. Don't think you always have to pay full price. In fact, most of the time, you don't!

Then there are entertainment clubs and loyalty groups that offer all kinds of discounts. Sometimes when you call your credit card company, at the end of your conversation, they will forward you to someone who offers you a "free trial" membership for a month in some kind of club where you'll get discounts on everything from shows to sporting events to gasoline. I've sometimes taken the free month, but then cancel for the paid subscription.

Summertime is Funnertime!

Most big cities hold tons of free events during the summer months. These include concerts, talks, readings, plays, workshops, jams, screenings, openings, and festivals. The outdoor concert, theater and movie season usually runs June through August with every imaginable kind of music, film and live stage happenings in parks, amphitheaters, and other open-air venues.

Events in many different cities can be found at **www.timeout.com** and **www.thrilllist.com**.

www.Eventbrite.com is another site where you'll find all kind of happenings going on in your neighborhood. On the left side of the site, they have listings by categories, including music, arts, parties, sports, the arts, food and drink, and networking. You can choose the date you're looking for as well as the event type, and most importantly, the price. Click on "FREE" and you'll find oodles of things to do without needing oodles of dough. (Unless you go to a cooking event, where dough might be provided!)

That's the beauty of the age we live in; you can discover what's going on in your city any day at the tip of your fingertips on the Internet. Take the opportunity to find out, and go out and treat yourself. You deserve it!

Thursday, Friday, Saturday and Sundays in Los Angeles are all big nights with popular bands and singers performing in various locations all over the city. Throngs of people come with blankets, picnics and friends to hear great music and have a blast.

www.SoCalSummerConcerts.com is a guide to free outdoor summer concerts around LA.

www.laweekly.com has listings of great events all year long.

So stop using being broke as an excuse to stay home. Get up, get out and have fun! Enjoy the nightlife, kick up your heels, and let loose. And live like a millionaire, even when you're a million short!

Chap Wrap 'n Recap

- Broadway Theater Lotteries
- Rush Seats and Hot Tix
- Discount Websites
- Half-price Ticket Booth
- Entertainment Book
- Movie Discounts
- Ushering
- Vegas, Baby!
- TV Shows and Seat Fillers
- Art Openings, Art Walks, and Museums
- Summer Concerts and Festivals

That's Entertainment Quiz – True or False

1. If I'm broke, all I can do is stay home and hack my neighbor's Wi-Fi.
2. In New York, Broadway shows will kill my wallet faster than a nasty divorce.
3. In Vegas, the only way to see a cheap show is to striptease in front of your mirror.
4. In the summer for free entertainment, make shadow puppets on your wall.
5. Wherever I am, I can have a blast for free.

3. So You Think You Can SHOP?!

"Whoever said money can't buy happiness, simply didn't know where to go shopping." –Bo Derek

What woman doesn't like shopping? Maybe there are a few, but none that I've known. Give a gal a credit card and set her free at a mall, chances are she will have a ball. Plenty of guys like to shop, too, though not all will admit it. Whether they're GQ studs or geekmeisters, there are a slew of men who crave designer clothes to grace their six-packs and hot booties or skinny abs and flat butts.

But what about us peeps who don't want to run up our bills on plastic? Or don't have the cash to splurge on new designer-duds-of-the-day? There are ways to shop that can keep more of your money in your wallet – and still leave you "lookin' fine!"

Clothes Make the Marilyn

My infatuation with clothes started when I was a little girl. I used to love Doris Day movies. Not only did she always get the guy; she always wore the most scrumptious outfits.

One of my favorite Doris Day movies was *A Touch of Mink*, with Cary Grant. (They had what's called a "cute meet." He splashes her when his luxury car is going around a corner, and her dress gets ruined.) My favorite scene in the movie was the one where he takes her to a chic clothing store, and high-fashion models come out parading in the latest stunning designer ensembles. Doris timidly points to the outfits she likes, and Cary BUYS them for her.

They did a scene like that in *Pretty Woman,* too, when Richard Gere's character takes Julia Robert's character into a store and he buys clothes for her. Of course, she was a hooker, but we ended up loving her anyway!

In any case, I just adore the idea of models posing in awesome clothes – and then a man telling the store owner to wrap them all up for *me!* So how come I never meet guys like that?

It turns out I don't need to, because I found other ways to get those coolest of cool clothes – without having to rely on a man. (Hey, if I lie on him once, and he's good, I will *re-lie* on him.) But I don't have to rely on him for buying me things. (Although, yes, I still think it would be verrrrrry nice if a man would buy me things, and expensive things, too!) For guys who are reading this book, know that they can *be* expensive things, but you *don't* have to spend a lot of money! It's a win-win for all.

> **Fashion Factoid: When you want to wear the clothes that bring you joy, know there's always a way.**

A Passion for Fashion

Shopping is a skill. It can be developed. But some of us have a natural talent for it. For me, it's a passion. And sometimes, just a pastime!

For instance, on a day when I'm feeling stressed or bored, instead of eating a pint of ice cream, which can be waaaay fattening – I just pick up and go shopping. Of course, that's more expensive than ice cream.

But it doesn't have to be. Just go to a store to "look", and you can even try on things. Hey, trying on clothes can be slimming, too. Try on enough, and it will burn calories. Besides which, if you don't like how you look, it can make you go on a diet!

A day of traipsing through the mall, trying on different clothes, can take you out of a bad mood and make you feel good. And if you find something you love, but it costs too much – don't worry, because I'm going to tell you *how and where* to find it for less!

Some people consider themselves "fashionistas." They dress to impress. They have a style. They start trends. They use the "Dress like everyone's watching" motto. "Functionistas", on the other hand, dress for function. Sometimes for fashion as well, but that is optional. (Not the same as "clothing optional." That means naked . . . and we won't go there.) There are times when fashionista and functionista overlap, and that's a time to celebrate. So I hope I inspire you to practice this with passion and joy while saving tons of money and looking absolutely fabulous.

> **"The journey of a thousand miles begins with . . . a really comfortable pair of shoes." –Lao Tzu . . . and ME!**

Are you a FASHIONISTA or a FASHION-UGGA?

Do you love to wear designer dresses? But all you can afford is burlap bags?

Would you like to know how you can wear a $2,000 dress for only $50, or a $3,500 dress for only $70?

Maybe you have an important occasion to go to and you want to look fabulous? Or maybe you just want to look great at the office, or at a party, or *on a hot date* – but you don't want to wear the same thing you wore two weeks ago.

Do you like Vera Wang or Nicole Miller or Kate Spade?

Well, you can wear a different designer every week . . . and not have to go over your budget!

How, you ask? Do what celebrities and stars do. When they go to an Awards Show or events, they don't *buy* their dresses – they just wear them that night, and then return them!

Now, I'm not suggesting you buy an expensive dress at a store and return it. (Although I know that some people do.) No, I'm suggesting you use a clothing rental store like **www.RentTheRunway.com**.

This is a terrific source that gives you a chance to dress like a millionaire – whether it's on one occasion . . . or a dozen.

You can rent a dress that retails for $2,000, pay only $50 – send it back, with free shipping – and get another one the next time you want to be a "fashionista."

So wear designer outfits – Carolina Herrera . . . Halston . . . Versace!

Besides dresses, they have handbags, jewelry and accessories. They carry things that retail from $100 to $8,000, with rental prices starting as low as $10 or $20.

You can do it for special occasions – or they even have an UNLIMITED OPTION where you pay by the month and you can get as many as you want, for only $139 a month!

Just think, you can wear new designer fashions every week, and not have a stuffed closet. Or a maxed-out credit card!

So try **www.RentTheRunway.com** – It's the Netflix of fashion!

By the way, they also have stores in some cities, including New York, Chicago, Washington DC, Las Vegas, and Woodland Hills, CA.

Other clothing rental sites:

> www.Closet.GwynnieBee.com
>
> www.LendingLuxury.com
>
> www.BagBorrowOrSteal.com
>
> www.LeTote.com
>
> www.StyleLend.com
>
> www.LightInTheBox.com
>
> www.GirlMeetsDress.com
>
> www.OneNightAffair.com

> **"I like my money right where I can see it: hanging in my closet."** –Carrie Bradshaw in Sex and the City

From Envy to On Me

Were you ever out at an event – and you saw someone wearing something that you loved? I was at this party and saw a woman wearing this amazing dress. I wanted it. I coveted it. I had to have it!

"I love your dress," I said. "Can I ask where you got it?"

She told me it came from a shop on Sunset Boulevard. I looked for the shop online – and wow, they were having a sale! I got in my car and zipped over there.

I tried on the dress and it looked gorgeous – but oh, no! It was the only thing there NOT on sale. (Grunt!) It was way over my budget at $800. Poor broke little me. But did I let it get me down? No way. In the dressing room, I looked at the name on the label. Hale Bob – a fantastic designer. I went home and got online. I found the dress on Zappos.com for half the price. Of course, I knew my size since I'd just tried it on and it looked like the bomb! Let's see, 365-day return policy. No shipping charges – "I'll buy it!"

But then, just in case, I looked on eBay. Wonder of wonders – it was on eBay. The same dress – in MY Size!

Now remember, for this you should know your size . . . and know it fits and looks great. I should have bought it at "buy it now" at $75. But I got into the auction and ended up getting it for $86. And at the original store it was $800!

The moral of story? – DO YOUR RESEARCH!

I've done this with designer shoes, too. Try them on at a store. Make sure they fit and you love them. Then go online to find them for less. I got a pair of $400 shoes for only $23!

Shop Till You Drop (The Price)

What else can you do when you see something in a store that you love, but can't afford? Believe it or not – there are ways to get it *at that store* for less!

In another chapter, I talk about **Rules to Live (Like a Millionaire) by**. The ones that are important to keep in mind when clothes shopping are:

1. Ask
2. Make Friends
3. Negotiate
4. Carpe Diem

1. The first rule is: Ask. "Will it go on sale?" "When?"

2. Make friends with the salesperson: Ask them to call you when it goes on sale.

3. Negotiate: If it has a missing button or a spot of dirt; or if it's the last one; or if it's been there a long time. Or tell them that another store has it for less. A lot of stores will match prices. You'd be surprised. Nordstrom, for instance. Isn't that amazing? Many people don't realize this. But if you see something you like at another store, or even online, often they will match the price.

4. Carpe Diem – Seize the Day! This applies when you see something that's at an incredible price, or if it's the last one there, or one-of-a-kind. Don't kick yourself the next day when you go back to the store and it's not there.

Also, if you buy it and don't wear it, take it back! At Nordstrom, they'll let you return it with no questions asked almost any time. A week later, a month later – or how's this for crazy – I knew a gal who took something back three years later!

The Case of the Coveted Cobalt Cashmere Coat

Ahhh, cashmere! It feels so good, but it can cost so much.

I was browsing through Nordstrom one day, when I saw it. This gorgeous cobalt blue blazer hanging at the front of a rack. It called out to me, "Marilyn! I'm here! Try me on!"

How could I resist? It was my size, and when I put it on, it looked sensational. But, whoaaa, the price tag read *$1,000*. No way could I justify spending that much! Did I pout? No. Did I walk away? No.

Instead, I approached the saleswoman. She immediately told me how fantastic the jacket looked on me. "Wow, that is *your* color," she said. I agreed, saying I loved it, but couldn't afford it. Then I asked her to call me and tell me if it went on sale. She said she'd be happy to do so.

A couple of weeks later, the salesgirl excitedly phoned me. "My" jacket was now $600. Nope, still too much!

A week later she called me again – "Your jacket is on a bigger sale: $400."

By the time I got to the store, it was on clearance . . . and it was the only one left. With my saddest puppy eyes, I told her it was still over my budget. "How about 200?" she asked. I countered, "How about 149?" She talked to her manager, and they agreed I could have it for the "Family and Friends" price: $149 for a $1,000-dollar jacket!

I'd *made friends* with this saleswoman, and she'd call me when all my favorite things went on sale. I always got incredible clothes there for incredible prices. I went back a few months later, but she'd been fired! (Uh-oh, I felt guilty, wondering if it was my fault. Hey, maybe she'd moved on to Saks?) But still, I'm advising you: Ask. Make friends. Negotiate. And buy that expensive item you want . . . *for less.*

Don't *Discount* Discount Stores

Don't be afraid to check out discount stores like Ross, Marshall's, Nordstrom Rack, DSW Shoes, etc. Gems await you.

Everything Old is New Again

> **"When you buy a piece of vintage clothing, you're not just buying the fabric and thread – you're buying a piece of someone's past." –Isabel Wolff**

Finding great vintage clothes can make you look like a million. I went into a store where a sign in the window proclaimed everything in the store was $5. I didn't think I'd find anything, but what the heck – I went inside to take a look.

Guess what! There was this great faux fur coat. Not only was it cool on the outside; it had a marvelous, multicolor lining. And fun colored buttons. And a faux fur ruffle. Oh, and it was actually a children's coat! But on me – it looked like a fabulous jacket. I bought it for $5 – and get compliments wherever I go!

Keep Your Eyes Peeled on the Road

Sometimes the best places to find awesome vintage bargains are not in your own city, but when you're traveling or on the go in not-so-big cities – or in areas where the word fashionista is foreign.

I was on the road between Los Angeles and San Francisco, going through a small beachside town, Morro Bay. I stopped for lunch, and while I was walking down the sidewalk, I saw a stylish red suede jacket hanging outside a thrift shop door. It was like brand new . . . and gorgeous! Even better, when I tried it on – it was MY size.

I was prepared to negotiate, since it looked like it must have cost $900 or more new. And it absolutely *looked* new. I got mentally ready to haggle back and forth. But when I asked how much, the answer was $15! OMG! I couldn't believe it. I bought it on the spot. Every time I wear it I get *tons* of compliments. Fifteen dollars! Whooooeeeee!

> "Buying something on sale is a very special feeling. In fact, the less I pay for something, the more it is worth to me. I have a dress that I paid so little for that I am afraid to wear it. I could spill something on it, and then how would I replace it for that amount of money?" – Rita Rudner

Be in Alignment with Consignment!

One of the best places for great deals is a **consignment shop**. For those of you who may be unfamiliar with these treasure troves, consignment shops accept used clothing and offer them for sale taking a percentage of the sales price for their services. Typically, they offer clothing for half price or less! You will often find them in or near the fairly affluent areas of a city. Often, you will find things that are practically new. The same rules apply as in all shopping, so please make friends with the salespersons.

Consign Online

Yep, these days you don't even have to go into stores to buy these treasures. What's more, you can sell your own clothes online, too. Try **www.ThredUp.com** which advertises "Second hand clothes, first hand fun." There are other websites, such as **www.Snobswap.com** and **www.Therealreal.com**. A number of young women have become their own fashion stores by setting up accounts on Instagram. It's a new world out there; we don't have to leave our homes to shop – but hopefully, you'll want to wear your fabulous finds *out in the world* for everyone to see!

> **"Anyone who lives within his means suffers from a lack of imagination." –Oscar Wilde**

How 'Bout FREE for You and ME?

How many of you have things in your closet that you bought and never wore? Or maybe only wore a few times? Or maybe it's been in your closet for one or two years and you haven't worn it since? You could try to sell it on eBay, but it's a pain in the neck to post it, and then you don't even know if it's going to sell. And if it does, you have to weigh it and ship it, and then the buyer might even return it! And then you have to repost it again. Ugh! It's not worth the time, and it's definitely not fun!

Instead, how about telling five women from the gym or eight friends from your book club, "Hey, let's have a Yankee Swap!"

A **Yankee Swap** is when you get a bunch of people together, and they all bring things in excellent or good condition that they never wear, and it's a party. Each of you brings your treasures, and you trade. Add some wine, and you have one helluva swapping par-tay! (Just clothes, not mates! Although *that* might be interesting, too.) You haven't lived till you've been at a party where women can try on things and get them for free. It's an awesome opportunity to get lots of new clothes, jewelry and accessories without spending a penny. I've been at parties where women have brought fabulous things. A terrific time to do this, with clothes and other items, is after the Christmas holidays. Because how many times do we get gifts that we don't like, and either you can't return them, or you don't know where they were bought, or you're too embarrassed to tell someone it doesn't fit, or you don't like their gift. So arrange a Yankee Swap, and get to pick out things you love. And how much do they cost? Nothing! Let me tell you, *that* is spelled pure F-U-N!

There are even ways to do swapping via the web: **www.SwapStyle.com** is a FREE online fashion swap marketplace. Women from all around the world swap their clothes online, and can save thousands of dollars in the process. You can also swap, buy and sell vintage, handmade, and second-hand designer fashions.

Another site is **www.RehashClothes.com**, where you can list the clothes, shoes, accessories, jewelry, and makeup you no longer want. You'll receive offers from other members. Once you accept an offer, you send your clothes and accessories to the other member, and you'll receive the items you've chosen. Rehash is free to use, with no listing fees or trading fees; you just pay your own shipping, and trade as much as you want.

www.MaterialWrld.com is a site that sends you a complimentary trade-in kit, and their shipping is always free. They make you an offer for your designer clothes, and you can use your earnings to shop online or in-store at places like Bloomingdale's, Nordstrom, Barneys, Neiman Marcus, Saks Fifth Avenue, and Saks OFF Fifth. I haven't tried it, but it sounds really cool.

> **"Never use the word 'cheap'. Today, everybody can look chic in inexpensive clothes (the rich buy them too). There is good clothing design on every level today. You can be the chicest thing in the world in a T-shirt and jeans — it's up to you."** –Karl Lagerfeld

Charity Stores

Salvation Army, Goodwill, and many other "charity" stores have long been places to find great treasures for a low price. Again, the stores near an affluent neighborhood will yield more of the greatest goodies, including many designer clothes. But you have to go often to find the best things, as their inventory changes daily, and the "gems" get gobbled up quickly. So be a smart shopper and you never know what you might find! My favorite charity thrift store is the Jewish Women's Council. They have them all over Los Angeles. It's a place where rich people donate, so they always have good things. Out of the Closet is another good store.

In addition to consignment stores or charity stores, there are other resale stores that offer designer clothes at discount prices. Check out the stores in your area.

In Los Angeles, you'll definitely want to check out "It's a Wrap." This is a store that carries clothes that were worn in movies or on TV. They have racks and racks from tons of popular shows; with each section indicating on what show they were worn. Just think, you could be wearing outfits that were on soap operas or sitcoms or in your favorite recent movie. They have a store in the Valley and one on the Westside. Check out their website at **www.itsawraphollywood.com**

> "You'd be surprised how expensive it costs to look this cheap." —Steven Tyler

Stay Loyal to Look Royal

Another thing many stores have started doing is offering what they may call "Loyalty Programs" or "Loyalty Points." When you sign up for the store's credit card, you get immediate discounts and points toward future discounts that can be quite good. Bloomingdale's does this, as do other department stores.

Wait for It to Go On Sale

Don't forget that sometimes, sales can be terrific. Macy's is a favorite of mine, because they have sales almost every weekend! In addition to regular sales, if you have a credit card there, they constantly mail you offers and extra discounts that are good through certain dates. I only shop at Macy's on Thursdays through Saturdays, when you get these extra discounts. The same items on Sundays through Wednesdays will cost you more, and I recommend you don't ever pay full price there. Also, keep in mind, in many stores, if something goes on sale within 10 days, or if you find it somewhere else for less, you can often get a price adjustment.

If the Shoe Fits – Buy It!

"I did not have three thousand pairs of shoes, I had one thousand and sixty." –Imelda Marcos

Imelda Marcos was a former First Lady of the Philippines who became infamous for her shoe collection. She had a rags-to-riches story that started with her living in poverty and not having enough money to buy shoes. So, when she married and became rich and famous, she bought thousands of designer shoes.

It's not a big revelation. Women love shoes. I think it's in their genes. I love them, but I can't wear them. That is, the stunning ones. The high heels. The stilettos. Not only can't I walk in them . . . I can't even stand in them. Because I have the world's worst feet. Great legs, but bad feet. They're totally flat – with bunions. (Just be glad this is a book and not a video!) In fact, as an aside, I keep getting calls from a clinical trial that wants to operate on my bunions . . . FOR FREE! But that's a different chapter ("Looking Good! Feeling Good!").

So, although I can go into the fanciest upscale stores and ogle the Christian Loubatins and Manolo Blahniks – I can't find any of them that I can wear. That saves me a bundle right there!

Some of today's other most coveted designer brands are Jimmy Choo, Louis Vuitton, Alexander McQueen, and Gucci. Retail prices for one pair of these top designer shoes can range anywhere from $600 to a whopping $10,000. Many styles are around the $1,000 to $2,000 range. Personally, I can't even understand why someone would *pay* $1,000 for a pair of shoes. But I'm not like most women, and I'm certainly not like any who are millionaires.

If *you* love top designer brands and can wear them – it's probable that you can't afford them at regular prices, either, at least not a whole closet full. Luckily, there are discount shoe stores where you can find them for less. Most of the websites for designer clothes have a shoe section as well. There are also sites that specifically feature shoes, including designer brands of various price levels. Check online for good deals, and remember to look for their extra discounts and sales. Many sites offer additional savings on your first order, or if you sign up for their mailing list.

Some sites to sample:

www.theoutnet.com

www.designerapparel.com

www.bluefly.com

www.shoeaholics.com

www.zappos.com

www.net-a-porter.com

www.shoebuy.com

Another way to find top designers at a discount is to buy pre-owned shoes.

www.unionandfifth.com

www.tradesy.com

Finally, if you love shoes but don't want to buy the most expensive brands, save your money and just admire them. A great inexpensive gift for yourself or any shoe-lover is *365 Days of Shoes Picture-A-Day Wall Calendar 2017.*

Whatever Your TAX Bracket – Pack a Jacket!

I'm the Imelda Marcos of jackets. Of course, I don't have one thousand and sixty jackets, or one thousand, or anywhere near that. Not 500, not even 300. Maybe 30 to 40 in my closet. Jackets are the one type of clothing I wear pretty much every day. Different styles and different colors, for my different moods. It's a simple style for me: black leggings and a black camisole, with a colorful jacket over them. When I want to dress up or show my shapely legs, I switch out the leggings for a short black skirt.

> **"You can spend a dollar on a jacket in a thrift store. And you can spend a thousand dollars on a jacket in a shop. And if you saw those two jackets walking down the street, you probably wouldn't know which was which." –Helen Mirren**

Yep, I love jackets. I had this red fleece jacket that had some patch designs on it that were artsy and fun. But they got old and faded. The natural thing to do would be to throw the jacket away. But not me, I wouldn't do that! I went to the fabric store and got some material with music notes on it. In another shop, I found a felt doo-dad shaped like a guitar, and at another place I got fabric decorated with piano keys. I don't sew (hard to believe, I know), so I took the jacket to a tailor and told him I wanted the pieces of fabric and felt guitar – sewn over the faded patches. I described exactly how I envisioned it, and a week later, VOILA, I had a new jacket. A new, super cool, eye-catching jacket. I get more compliments on that jacket than on almost anything else I own!

Fix It and Mix It

You can be creative, too. Stores like Michael's and Jo-Ann Fabric and Crafts have all kinds of craft goodies from sequins to beads to patches and fringe. You can affix things to plain clothes – or if, like me, you can't sew, just take them to a tailor and tell him what you want. You'll have something truly special.

I had this hot pink jacket that I loved, loved, loved – and wore to death. Whenever I did a TV show or an in-person event, I wore it. I had to stop, because people thought I had just one thing in my closet. But I loved that jacket sooooo much – as well as the way it fit – I decided to try to get a dressmaker to make it for me in other colors. So I went to Craigslist and Angie's List to find them.

I interviewed a few, and found one who said she was a jacket specialist! She said she made jackets for famous performers like Ozzie Osbourne (the English rock star whose wife, Sharon Osbourne, is on *The Talk*.) Anyhow, the dressmaker took my hot pink jacket and made a pattern out of it. We got silk fabric in a different color, a bold RED, and she made me a jacket. I was going to get two more, in Kelly green and royal blue. (If you haven't figured it out yet, I like bright colors – I'm a "winter.")

Unfortunately, the dressmaker took a lot longer to make it than she said she would. I wanted it by Thanksgiving, but it still wasn't ready by Christmas. And when I went for a fitting, one sleeve was LONGER than the other, so she had to redo it. Two weeks after New Year's it still wasn't right. Finally, after Valentine's Day I got the finished red jacket. She felt so bad that it took so long – and that she'd had to keep redoing it – that she gave me the jacket, just for the price of the pattern! (And for $800 less than it would cost at a store).

I still have that nice red jacket, although I never went back for the green or blue. But I still have the pattern, so one never knows! I just might add another color to my jacket collection one day.

Bottom line: you can get someone to make something for you that *looks* like it cost big bucks, but that's been custom made for you. But be prepared: it may take longer than they say . . . and you might end up with one sleeve longer than the other. (As long as they match your arms!)

Keep Me in Stitches

Handmade items are always special. If you're a good seamstress, or if you're fortunate enough to have a mother, grandma, or aunt (or father, grandpa or uncle) who sews or knits, you can be a fashion plate with economical one-of-a-kind outfits.

When I was a little girl, I took tap dancing lessons and my mother would make all my costumes for my recitals. She made a chartreuse-colored mouse suit for me to wear, to play one of the mice in *Cinderella*. Then, when I was a teenager and started ice skating, she'd sew colorful skating skirts and vests for me with matching pom-poms for my skates. By the time I was in college, Mom was on a knitting craze. She made me a stunning turquoise and olive two-piece suit with a coat and skirt. The only problem was, as the years went by and styles changed, I'd keep asking her to shorten it, more and more. She'd unravel the hem time after time until, finally, I had a mini-skirt . . . and she had enough wool left to make a whole new suit!

If you are sewing-challenged and none of your relatives or good friends are creative, you can check out sites like www.etsy.com and www.scoutmob.com for handcrafted and homemade items.

Altered States and Altered Greats

Don't forget, you can always go to a dressmaker to fix that dress you found that's too big or to alter that skirt you bought two years ago that needs to be shorter now. Getting last season's clothes fixed often costs less than buying something new. The trick is to find a tailor or dressmaker who does great work at a great price. It's even better if you have a loving granny with a trusty sewing machine! "Oy, you want me to make it so short?"

One Celeb's Shopping Shtick

If you want to live the true millionaire lifestyle, take Barbra Streisand's lead and build your own shopping mall in your basement! That's right, Babs has a complete mall in her basement, with clothes boutiques and other shops.

"Instead of just storing my things in the basement, I can make a street of shops and display them," Streisand says. Before she goes out, she calls down to the clerk, and has him pull out the outfit she wants to wear.

Streisand's coffee table book, *My Passion for Design,* includes a chapter devoted to her underground arcade. There's even a hit play, *Buyer and Cellar,* that is all about Barbra Streisand's basement:

www.bbc.com/news/entertainment-arts-31904284

"And now, I'm just trying to change the world, one sequin at a time." –Lady Gaga

Other Resources

www.NordstromRack.com

www.Lastcall.com

www.Hautelook.com

www.BarneysWarehouse.com

www.6pm.com

www.Ideel.com

www.Gilt.com

www.Loehmanns.com

www.LuxuryGarageSale.com

www.zappos.com

www.Ruelala.com

www.FilenesBasement.com

www.Shopedropoff.com

www.Yoox.com

www.Zulilly.com

www.InaNYC.com

www.Nuji.com

So now I've given you a ton of wise ways to get fabulous clothes at fabulous prices. Let your Inner Millionaire shine through, and have some truly dynamite things that bring you joy and make you feel good. Then, when you want *new* things, have a Yankee Swap, or sell your stuff on consignment or eBay . . . and start all over again!

"Dress shabbily and they remember the dress; dress impeccably and they remember the woman." –Coco Chanel

Chap Wrap 'n Recap

- Don't Buy – Rent!
- Comparison Shop
- Ask, Make Friends, Negotiate
- Go Vintage
- Go Online
- Realign and Consign
- Wait for Sales
- Discount Stores and Sites
- Hop to a Swap
- Shoes-a-Palooza
- Don't Falter – Alter!

So You Think You Can SHOP Quiz – Fill in the Blank

You can get expensive designer clothes by getting _____ to buy them for you.

1. A fool
2. Some rich guy
3. Your husband
4. Your mother
5. All of the above
6. None of the above

A Yankee Swap is:

1. When Confederate soldiers got prisoners back from Union soldiers
2. When a British person French-kisses someone from the USA
3. A reggae rap group with their own show on MTV
4. A long red, white, and blue scarf worn around the hips
5. A party where gals get together and joyfully trade clothes

Imelda Marcos is:

1. A fashion designer who makes costumes for Jennifer Lopez
2. The owner of a boutique that carries gowns made by Britney Spears
3. A fashion icon who wore bullet bras before Madonna started the trend
4. A Spanish hat designer who created headdresses for Carmen Miranda
5. The widow of a dictator in the Philippines, known for her thousands of shoes

You can rent a fabulous designer dress and then return it at:

1. Rent-what-you-can't-afford.com
2. Rent-at-amway.com
3. Rent-the-tramway.com
4. Rent-in-a-chummy-way.com
5. RentTheRunway.com

4. Eats, Treats, and Feats

"As a child, my family's menu consisted of two choices: Take it or leave it." –Buddy Hackett

Foodie Adventures – Ways to Eat Great for Less!

ARE YOU A FOODIE? I am. I love to eat. But I hate to cook. In fact, whenever I meet a guy, I tell him: "No man's mother will ever be jealous that I cook better than her."

I've definitely lived up to that. I was with my ex-boyfriend for many years, and he did all the cooking. Then one night, after five years, I decided to give him a surprise and make dinner for him. It was from a yummy recipe my Aunt Elaine used to make – sweet and sour meatballs. I was excited. I was going to show him I could create a dish worthy of Julia Child . . . if she were Swedish! But uh-oh, while opening a can of tomato sauce, I cut my finger, and blood started spurting everywhere. Not to mention tomato sauce. Eeek, the wall looked like a Jackson Pollack painting! My boyfriend sprang into action and drove me to the emergency room, where I got five stitches.

When we left the hospital, we were both starved – so he had to take me out to dinner. Then, when we got home, he had to clean up the tomato sauce stains all over the kitchen. And, of course, I couldn't help because I had a bandaged and sewed-up sore finger. The best part was that I was officially off the hook as far as being a cook. He begged me never to go into the kitchen again!

Anyhoo, since I love to eat and hate to cook, it means I go out to eat most of the time. As you can imagine, that can get expensive, really expensive! But, you probably know by now – for me, it doesn't.

"Nothing would be more tiresome than eating and drinking if God had not made them a pleasure as well as a necessity." –Voltaire

There are many different and delightful ways to eat out at all kinds of restaurants in your neighborhood (or on your travels), without paying regular restaurant prices.

Coupons, Groupons and *You*-pons!

www.Restaurant.com lists more than 18,000 restaurants all over the country – which means there's probably one in your neighborhood, or wherever you're traveling, with just the kind of food you love. They have restaurants in Los Angeles, New York, Chicago, Baltimore, New Orleans – well, all over the country. You sign up for free – and then you buy restaurant certificates at a discount, and use them as cash. You can buy certificates worth $10, $25, or $100 at various restaurants.

Usually, you'd buy a $25 certificate for $10. So you'd be saving $15. But what I like to do is wait for their sales. By email, they tell you – "Today, a $25 certificate is only $4." Or sometimes, it's even $2, or $1. And wow, then you're getting a real bargain. So I stock up on them when they go on sale.

Please note, when you buy the certificate, it indicates the *minimum purchase* you must make at that specific restaurant. For instance, if you buy a $25 certificate, you may have to make a *minimum purchase* *of $37.50* when dining. This means you'll have to pay an additional $12.50 at the restaurant. (Doing the math, if you bought a $25 certificate for $2, you'll actually spend a total of $14.50 to get a meal worth $37.50.) On a $100 certificate, there might be a *minimum purchase of $150.* (So, if you buy a $100 certificate for $25, then you'll have spent $25 + $50, i.e. $75 for a meal worth $150.)

Now, I'm not an accountant, but I know you are getting terrific savings at these restaurants. It's great for trying out a new eatery for the first time. Then, if you like it, you can buy more certificates for return visits. The certificates are also wonderful for giving as gifts.

> **"Some people ask me for the secret of our long marriage. We take time to go to a restaurant two times a week. A little candlelight, dinner, soft music and dancing. She goes Tuesdays, I go Fridays." –Henny Youngman**

www.Groupon.com and **www.LivingSocial.com**. Both of these websites offer excellent bargains on restaurants. Sometimes it will be a dinner for two that's worth $130 for only $60. Or it might be a $30 meal for $15 or a five-course dinner with wine for $39.

Check the sites to see what they offer in your city.

Again, you can find locations all over the country. Here you buy the vouchers for cash, and then use them when you go to the restaurant for your meal. There is an expiration date for each of these promotions, but you never lose the amount you paid, i.e. if you can't get to the restaurant before the expiration date on the deal, you still get the value of the money you actually paid.

Insider Tip

Pay attention to your emails from these sites. Why? They frequently offer discounts on their discounts! Every so often they will give you codes to get 20 percent off or an extra $10 to $30 off, and then the deals are even better! When I get these emails, I stock up on the Groupons or Living Social certificates. With an extra 20 percent OFF, that $130 dinner listed for $60 will cost only $48. Or with the extra $10 discount, the $39 five-course dinner with wine will be only $29. Such a deal! And such a meal!

www.Blackboardeats.com. This is a website that offers restaurant deals in New York, Los Angeles, San Francisco, and Chicago as well as some national deals. The nice thing about Blackboard Eats is that, not only is it free to sign up, but it's free to get your discounts. You don't pay anything in advance. They send you periodic emails telling you a restaurant is going to offer you a 30 percent discount (or some other deal), and if you click on it, you get a passcode to use when you go there. So, for this site, you pay no money upfront. You just have to get your code within the promotional period and visit the restaurant before the specified deadline. Also, they often give extra discounts and expanded deadlines if you happen to be a Citicard member.

The Entertainment Book. This is a coupon book which has been around for a long time in many cities. It generally costs $35 to $40 and is often sold by charities as well as online or at some bookstores. They offer many 2-for-1 or deep discount coupons for restaurants and many other "entertainment" events, as well as travel deals and retail offers. The other way to save on this, is that after July 1st they sell that year's book for only $8! You can more than make that up the first time you use the book! Check them out at **www.entertainment.com.**

Some other sites that give restaurant deals include **www.yipit.com and www.yelp.com.**

Many people don't know that AAA, Bank of America, and even Verizon Wireless offer discounts on many things, including restaurants. If you are a member, check their websites to find out what the benefits are; you may be surprised.

Also, keep in mind, most restaurants have a **birthday program** where you eat free on your birthday, or on a day during the month of your birthday. Whether you have friends to go with you, or you just want to get out of the house yourself, it's a complimentary meal at a place that you like. Make a month of it with a different restaurant every day. They often send you other discounts throughout the year, too!

So start going out to great restaurants, at great prices! Check out Restaurant.com, Groupon.com, Living Social.com, Blackboardeats.com and the Entertainment Book. They all have apps, too. And don't forget to bring your appetites! I've got my coupons ready. Now let's eat!

> **"Take life with a grain of salt . . . a slice of lime, and a shot of tequila!"** –Unknown

Be a Foodie Friend!

One other tip with regard to these sites: if you refer a friend, they often give you a $10 credit on your account. Your besties will thank you for sharing the savings, and you'll both be feasting for less. So keep referring your friends, and watch *your* free meals add up!

Don't Worry, Be Happy . . . at Happy Hour

Do you have expensive taste when it comes to taste? Do you like high class restaurants – but not high class prices? Would you be happy if you could go to really expensive restaurants, really *in*expensively? The secret of happiness: try *happy hours*!

As I've already confessed, I'm the world's worst cook. So I eat out a lot. And I love really good restaurants. But going out to eat at them could cost a small fortune.

I'll give you some examples:

Ruth's Chris Steak House – it has wonderful atmosphere and wonderful food. But you pay for it! At dinner, a steak costs anywhere from $39 to $48. And that's just the entrée. A crab cake appetizer is $19.00. And then there are drinks and dessert: $100 a person, or $200 for two people. I go to Ruth's Chris Steak House all the time – for happy hour. They have great food choices for $9 – Prime burger with Fries: $9. Tenderloin skewer with salad: $9. Crab BLT with zucchini fries: $9. Ahi tuna; a steak sandwich; spicy lobster. Any one of them = only $9. You still get the great food and the atmosphere, but not the high prices.

Another one is: **Fleming's Steak House** – Their steaks are from $40 to $59. Yikes! Another meal for $70 to $100 a person or more! But they have a happy hour from 5 to 7 p.m. – where they give you five different food choices – each for $6. I had a delicious flatbread with filet mignon on it. OMG, it was TDF (To Die For.) They also have a *later* happy hour from 8 to 10 p.m. You can get eight different dishes – for $9 each! Try short ribs, tuna tacos, all kinds of things.

And also: **McCormick & Schmick's** – Dinner entrees there are about $20 to $40. But at happy hour, they have food from $2.99 to $5.99.

I picked these restaurants as examples, because they have them all over the country. But if you have an upscale eatery in your neighborhood that you think you can't afford, check to see if they have a happy hour. It might be from 4 to 7 p.m., or a late night happy hour. Oh yeah, if you drink, drinks are cheaper too! But I'm a foodie, so I'm more interested in the snacks and eats.

And remember, when you go, if they have a mailing list – make sure to sign up. They may send you specials. For instance, you might get a free meal on your birthday!

So go ahead, get happy at happy hour!

> "I drink to make other people more interesting." – Ernest Hemingway

Munch a Bunch at Lunch 'n Brunch

In addition to happy hours, a restaurant's **lunch menu** is often less expensive than their dinner menu. So you can go for a wonderful lunch at a reasonable price. Also, some places have **early bird prices**, or even a **tea-time menu**.

> "I went to a restaurant that serves 'breakfast at any time'.
> So I ordered French Toast during the Renaissance."
> –Steven Wright

I loved a couple of the trendy restaurants on Abbot Kinney Boulevard in Venice, CA, but their dinner prices were too high for me, with entrees from $20 to $30. Add a drink and dessert, and it would cost me $50 every time I went. But they offered a **Weekend Brunch** with an appetizer, entrée and dessert all included for $12 to $15. And sometimes, these brunches include a mimosa or a drink. My friends and I loved going there Saturdays or Sundays. It was waaaaay cheaper than dinnertime, and still tasted deelish.

In addition, I usually can't finish my whole meal, so I will share a dish with a friend. Or better still, I'll order a meal and take half of it home in a doggie bag. (Woof, woof, that's me – the next day!) So, even though it may cost more than you'd spend for one meal, it may not be so expensive when you think of it as two meals. One other thing: you can always order your favorite dish to take out from a restaurant, thereby saving what you'd have to spend on a tip if you were eating there.

Eating Around the World . . . in Your Own Back Yard

Another way to have outstanding food at reasonable prices is to **go ethnic.** Many cities have specific areas filled with local ethnic eateries that are excellent – and totally special. Whether you're in Los Angeles, Chicago, New York or New Orleans, or anywhere in between, check out the neighborhoods that feature a number of restaurants with a particular kind of cuisine. In Los Angeles, Little Osaka, near Sawtelle and Olympic Streets in West LA, has a ton of delightful and unique Asian restaurants serving everything from sushi to ramen, Japanese curries and spaghetti, Asian barbecue and more – and it's all authentic. And economically priced!

Many cities have a Chinatown where they feature dim sum and other genuine Chinese dishes. There's also Ethiopia Town, and Korea Town, in Los Angeles. In New York, there's Little Italy for Italian, and Little Odessa for Russian food. The Big Apple can be a devastatingly expensive place to visit, but it doesn't have to be. Check out some of the really cool little eateries in neighborhoods not so often frequented by tourists. Once, in New York City we stayed at a B&B and took a walk around the corner to find throngs of people lined up at a bunch of Indian restaurants. It turns out this area of Murray Hill is fondly called "Curry Hill." It's almost like you are in another country when you find a special place with authentic cuisine from another country. So eat like you're traveling the world, except no passport needed!

> **"I've been taking diet pills . . . I don't eat less, I just eat faster."** –Marilyn Anderson

Grand Openings

Watch for any new restaurants, hotels or casino openings. Before they open for business, these establishments often have a "practice night." You can go and get everything free! This is not public knowledge, but a little schmoozing with any of the staff, and you can discover what night to attend and leave your wallet at home!

But How, You Ask?

Last summer, a shopping center in my neighborhood was being renovated, and a lot of new restaurants were opening. I was walking out from a movie one night and noticed that Ruth's Chris Steak House was going to be opening. I knew this was a high-quality – and expensive – chain of eateries throughout the country.

What I also knew was that before restaurants open their doors to the public, they want their new staff to be ready and on their toes. So, they most often have one or two nights for their servers to practice.

These might be called "Practice Nights" or sometimes "Friends and Family" nights. But the best part of these nights is that they are *FREE* to the diners. The secret is how to get on their list. And it may be different for each new restaurant.

I saw that Ruth's Chris was going to be opening, so I called them and asked if they were going to have a practice night. They responded, "It's tomorrow night. But it's for VIPs and important people."

I responded, "I'm an important person."

Guess what! They asked for my name and put me on the list! I invited two friends and, OMG – what a night we had!

Upon our arrival, the hostess welcomed us and took us to a plush red booth, where we were offered our choice of cocktails. Then our server gave us the menu where we got to choose any appetizer we each wanted and a selection of scrumptious steaks, seafood, and entrees from their menu. We also ordered side dishes, wine, and delectable desserts.

For this opening, they even had a New Orleans Jazz Band, and all the guests were invited to form a line and samba through the kitchen to wave to the chef and staff.

The evening was completely complimentary. (And probably would have cost about $400!) It was amazing. My male friend was a true gentleman, and left the servers a nice tip. But let me tell you, it was one awesome evening. Another hint I learned when I was there was that, although their dinners are very expensive – they were going to be offering terrific bargains at their happy hour!

I've been at grand openings for numerous other restaurants. Sometimes, I'll hear about it from a friend. Once, because I was on the email list for a restaurant with several locations, I got a personal invitation that they were opening a new one in a different neighborhood, and they were doing a "Family and Friends" night, so I could bring up to three guests for a five-course dinner there . . . all complimentary.

So make sure you get on those **mailing lists!** Or, if you see a new place that's going to open, go in and introduce yourself as someone who goes out to eat often, or offer them a Yelp review, or say you're a VIP! You may just get to treat yourself and your guests to a sensational dinner on the town.

Food Fests and Tastings

Many cities have various festivals to celebrate their foods and restaurants. Whether it's a festival or a "Taste of," these are a great way to sample the cuisine from many expensive restaurants at a low price. Sometimes it's a "one price covers all," but at other times, the events have tickets that you buy and spend on the food. Dishes and beverages might cost anywhere from three to seven tickets, depending on the particular foods that each restaurant offers. In any case, there is always a festive atmosphere, and it's a fun way to take a culinary tour of the local scene.

Conserve Water – Drink Beer

If you have a food or beverage manufacturer in your town, check to see if they have a tour. For example, in Los Angeles, there is the Golden Road Brewery. Visiting is informative, and you get free samples of the freshest beer that you will ever taste. My friend John once toured the Jack Daniel's distillery in Tennessee. He was enjoying the tour, and expecting to have some tasty samples at the end of the tour. When none were offered, he inquired, and was told that it is a "dry county," and therefore illegal to give or even sell alcohol there. He was kind of shocked and disappointed, but got over it a few blocks away where it was a different county. John and "Jack" became great friends!

It's Wine O'clock

All wineries usually offer tastings, which give you a sampling of their wine, either free or at low cost. They are fun, especially with a group of friends. When you visit a place like Napa Valley in California, there are tons of wineries near each other, and they all give samples. Pick a designated driver and go wine-tasting for the day! Many of these places also offer crackers and cheese or other tidbits to go with their wine samples, and to cleanse your palate between different selections. Hmmm, a little wine tour is a great way to spend a day . . . and feel like you're living the life!

> "In wine there is wisdom, in beer there is freedom, in water there is bacteria." –Benjamin Franklin

See Where It's Made – and Feed Your Face, Too!

Many food and beverage manufacturers offer tours of their facilities. These are frequently free to visitors, who are always given free samples. Almost every state has a slew of different tours available from soup to nuts, or coffees to candies. Needless to say, families and kids love places with sugary treats: some tasty ones are the Jelly Belly, Hershey's Chocolate, and Ben & Jerry's Ice Cream tours. Check out factories near you and feed your sweet tooth – just don't tell your dentist! (The U.S. Mints in various cities offer tours for visitors, too – but unfortunately, there are no free samples there!) An excellent site listing tours throughout the country is **www.factorytoursusa.com.**

One of the most offbeat and unknown food and beverage fests is the National Restaurant Association Show in Chicago each May. They have celebrity chefs, and just about every food and beverage manufacturer is represented. They have all kinds of delicious food and every kind of beverage that you can imagine, all free! I even met Orville Redenbacher, the king of popcorn, there. You have to be over 16, and in the hospitality business; but aren't we all? Make yourself a business card on your computer and try to go: **http://show.restaurant.org/**

Do you Eat to Live or Live to Eat?

Investment seminars are often held at nice restaurants where the guests get a complimentary dinner and learn about investments . . . without necessarily buying anything. I've had some great meals at fantastic restaurants, and all I had to do was listen to the sales pitch. It was fun, and I met some handsome guys, too!

My Dinner with Wolfgang

Wolfgang Puck has become famous as a celebrity chef. He has numerous restaurants across the globe. I've been to a few, but the way I got to go to a wonderful one in my neighborhood was particularly interesting and shows how you, too, can . . . not only *eat* like a millionaire . . . but eat WITH millionaires.

I was listening to a radio station, and they were touting a particular financial company that would send information on how to grow your money. It sounded intriguing to me, so I went to their site and signed up to get their newsletter.

A few weeks later, I got an invitation in the mail for an investment seminar at Wolfgang Puck's restaurant, *Chinois on Main*. I was invited to bring a friend and come for dinner. I called two or three girlfriends, but no one wanted to join me. Whatever! I decided to go by myself, and I was soooo glad *they* stayed home.

I got to the restaurant, and the event was in a private room. I was greeted by a server with a tray of wine glasses. Already I realized, *Mmmm, this is going to be a lovely evening!* Smiling, I selected a glass of Cabernet Sauvignon and started demurely sipping it. People were mingling (mostly men, I will add) and chatting about this and that.

We were invited to sit down at banquet tables and enjoy a four-course meal with appetizers, entrees, dessert, and champagne. Before the dessert, they gave a 20-minute presentation about "Life Settlements." It was very informative and interesting, and something I knew nothing about. They were seeing if any of the invited guests would be interested. Some were, some weren't, but the bottom line is we were all definitely enjoying the delicious cuisine and wonderful ambience.

As it turned out, I was the only woman at our table, and I was eating a luscious gourmet meal with five interesting possible millionaires. (Of course, some of the guys could have been like *me*, and just enjoying the experience. But the ones truly interested in the products the financial company had to offer were definitely heavy in the wallet.)

I had the best time. I actually went out on a few dates with one of the men who *DID* invest in their products. Though I didn't invest, I *did* get invited by the company to several more elite events, which were always high class, and filled with thought-provoking information and intriguing guests.

"You are what you eat!" –Anthelme Brillat-Savarin

A lot of baby boomers will probably get invited to many investment seminars. Some of these may be at mid-range restaurants like Marie Callender's or Olive Garden; but you never know, you might just find yourself at another one of Wolfgang Puck's elegant eateries, sitting with some millionaires. And if a friend invites you, think before you say no. You will definitely enjoy it, plus you'll be learning about investments, even if "now" might not be the time to make one. And you might even meet a millionaire there. Or how about a BILLIONAIRE? Sounds good to me!

Eating Out, Treating In

Speaking of Wolfgang Puck, I recently got an invite through Facebook about a new dine-in delivery service that features meals prepared by famous chefs. On the FB ad, it indicated you could have your first meal *absolutely free*. It was because they were newly introducing their service to the Los Angeles area.

www.Munchery.com in New York, San Francisco and Los Angeles features daily delivery service straight to your home, with gourmet cuisine from well-known chefs working at posh restaurants.

On Facebook, I got a special code to use, looked at the menu for the day – and chose an entrée and dessert. That evening, at the specified time, the delivery arrived at my door. And it was true: my first meal was absolutely complimentary. Simple heating directions were included for my yummy gourmet salmon with pesto and vegetables. The dinner tasted like one I would get at a fancy restaurant; I totally enjoyed it . . . and I never even had to leave home.

Don't Keep Your Secrets *Secret!*

What's more, I was given a referral code to tell my friends about it. If they ordered, they would get a $20 discount, and I would get $20 in my Munchery account. You can bet I sent the link to a bunch of friends. Not just because of the discounts, but because the meal was excellent, and sometimes I just don't feel like going out. How wonderful to have a gourmet meal brought right to your door! A few days later, a friend told me she'd ordered from them and loved it. Oh, and yeah – I now have $20 towards my dinner the next time I feel like just chillin' at home and eatin' like a princess in front of the TV by myself.

Here's my code for you to get $20 off:

www.munchery.com/invite/GC77HBYH

"One of the very nicest things about life is the way we must regularly stop whatever it is we are doing and devote our attention to eating." –Luciano Pavarotti

There are many new meal delivery places now, including some specifically geared to healthy eating. Many will give discounts the first time you try them; others are listed on Groupon and Living Social. Googling "meal delivery" in your city will turn up all kinds of choices. Most of these will be for weekly or monthly meal plans, which are great if you don't like to cook, but like to eat at home. In Los Angeles, some of them are Wholesome2go.com, Freshology.com, BlueApron.com,

HomeChef.com, CaliforniaChef.com, Paleta.com, Sakara.com and many more. There's now even UberEats.com to get food delivered from your favorite restaurant whenever you want.

I like to pick up takeout from some expensive restaurants that I wouldn't necessarily go to myself. Often they will give big portions, and then I can make two or three meals out of it! What's more, if you're taking it out, you don't have to leave a tip.

Speaking of Facebook . . .

A good idea is to "like" your favorite restaurants on their Facebook fan page. Sometimes they will have offers or freebies for their fans. In addition, don't forget, when you go to restaurants at happy hour or lunch – to put your business card in their bowl. They often have giveaways where you may get a free lunch for four or a dinner for two. And sign up on their email list for special deals and discounts. You may want to create a designated email address dedicated to deals and offers from restaurants and other merchants – so it doesn't tie up your business or personal email accounts.

I Heard It Through the Grapevine . . . I Mean, On the Radio

Sometimes, you can get terrific deals on restaurants during **membership drives** or **charity events**, either in person, or on the radio. An example: every year, I become a member of KCRW radio station. They have many fabulous restaurants giving you dinner for two when you donate $50 to $100 to the radio station during their drive. So, even though it's a nonprofit, and you get a tax deduction, you get a delightful dinner to go along with your donation.

In addition, when you're a member of KCRW, you can get free movie tickets at different times during the year; also, every night, they have a giveaway of some fantastic concert, event or show. If you call in and win, these can sometimes be worth $200 – and you sometimes get them for free when you become a member.

So, for the price of becoming a member (anywhere from $50 and up), you can get a free dinner for two, plus free tickets to a concert or show up to four times a year. (They only allow you to win once every three months.) *And* you're helping your favorite radio station at the same time! Along with your membership, you also get a bunch of other discounts at restaurants and retail shops all year long. Offers are listed on their website.

Nosh 'n Blog It!

Okay, let's not leave out the one way you can get lots of free meals at lots of cool restaurants all over: by **becoming a food reporter or blogger**. If you are a foodie, and like to write about it, you can start your own blog and get it noticed by lots of followers. If you get a really big following, then the restaurants will want you to come and write about them.

Was the Food Bitchin' or Were YOU Bitchin'?

There's another way to get a great meal and great service at a chic restaurant. If you've been to a place, maybe with a rich friend or business associate, and the service was bad or the food wasn't up to par, or you found a fly in your soup, you can write a respectful letter of complaint. If it's really true, and you tell them in a nice way and specifically indicate what you had and what was wrong, many restaurants will send you a gift certificate to return and have a better experience.

I've done this several times when it was justified, and received anywhere from a $50 gift certificate to a $100 gift certificate. However, I only do it if there is a good reason. Besides, you don't want to get a reputation for doing it everywhere over and over. You don't want them whispering in the kitchen, "Oh, no, here comes that kvetching bitch again! Let's spit in her food!"

Chap Wrap 'n Recap

- Happy Hours and Lunch or Brunch
- Coupons for Cuisine
- Entertainment Book
- Going Ethnic
- Openings and Tastings
- Investment Seminars
- Food Festivals
- Sharing or Splitting
- Bitching and Kvetching

A Quiz for Foodies – True or False

When I want to eat out at an expensive restaurant, I:

1. Look through the window at the diners and salivate
2. Hang outside the back door and look for scraps in the dumpster
3. Take money out of my IRA
4. Go for happy hour or lunch
5. Buy a Groupon
6. Go to Restaurant.com

"You are what you eat! Are you a steak? Or a hot dog? As for me, I'm a hot tomato!" –Marilyn Anderson, Author, *Women Who Are Hungry for Love, and the Men Who Always Eat First!*

5. Looking Good! Feeling Good!

"Beauty is only skin deep, but ugly is to the bone." – Dorothy Parker

We all like to look good. But the price of beauty these days can be high. Hell, it can be astronomical! Just the normal things, like getting our hair done, our nails done, makeup, our legs waxed, bikini waxes, it all costs money. A makeover used to mean changing your foundation powder and the color of your lipstick and eye shadow. Now it's full face transformations with nose jobs, eye jobs, brow lifts, Botox injections, lip plumping, cheek lifts, chin reductions, and so forth. Not to mention moving down from the chin to boob jobs, liposuction, fanny padding, and more. But let's not even go into the plastic surgery stratosphere. Just for the simplest things like hair and makeup – beauty can cost women a small, no make that a *huge* fortune every year. It's no surprise that beauty is a multi-million-dollar business, because women want to look beautiful and are willing to pay for it. And that goes for men, too.

"Gorgeous hair is the best revenge." –Ivana Trump

The good news about looking good today is that there are all kinds of ways to do it without having to spend a king's ransom. Salons, stylists and spas of all kinds are offering a myriad of discounts to attract clients. Which means you will have your choice of many places to make you look more beautiful, whether it's for your hair, nails, hands, feet, face, skin or your bodacious bod.

Here are a few online sites you should check out immediately and often: Groupon.com, LivingSocial.com, GiltCity.com and Yipit.com.

www.Groupon.com and **www.LivingSocial.com** are both websites with tons of great offers in many categories, including those dealing with beauty and health where you can search for appointments, browse deals, and book services from top health and beauty businesses in your city. They have discounts and deals on hair services, eyelashes, massages, waxing, facials, injectables, nails, and tanning from salons and boutiques in various neighborhoods. Besides their listed discounts, they frequently offer even deeper discounts by allowing you to take 10 to 30 percent more off the original listing.

www.GiltCity.com is another website with a **Relaxing and Pampering** section featuring deals and offers from salons, stylists and services in various cities, including New York, Los Angeles, Atlanta, Boston, Chicago, Dallas, Houston, Philadelphia, San Diego, San Francisco, Seattle and Washington DC, as well as some national deals.

Then there's **www.Yipit.com**, which offers bargains and discounts for beauty deals all over by compiling offers from assorted sites. So there's *no reason to ever pay full price* to make yourself look grand.

And remember, once you've joined these sites for free, if you refer your friends, you'll get credits on your account, which also add up to YOU looking your best at amazingly low prices. Here's an example of my referral code: use it to get your discounted offers, and I'll get $10 in my account for helping YOU save money. Plus, *you* get an extra discount, too. Then YOU can get a referral code when you recommend it to your friends. It's a win-win-win-win for everyone!

https://www.groupon.com/visitor_referral/h/21d6cc0e-c29d-492b-8034-11273db02b47

"People always ask me how long it takes to do my hair.
I don't know, I'm never there." –Dolly Parton

Now let's get to some of the other specifics on *How to Live Like a MILLIONAIRE*: with dazzling hair, nails, skin, and overall pampering in which you can luxuriate.

Hair Apparent – What Me, Model?

"If they ever do my life story, whoever plays me needs lots of hair color and high heels." –Charlize Theron

It can be expensive being a woman, because every time you want to go to a salon to get your hair done, it can cost $60, $100, or even $300. That's more than I have in my budget, and maybe it's more than you have in yours. That's why I go, and recommend that you go, to become a *hair model*. "Now, wait a minute," you say. "What if I'm not gorgeous? Or thin ? Or young?"

Well, the good thing about being a hair model is you only need *one thing* – HAIR! The stylists have to do all kinds of hair. And not just women's hair. This is for men, too. For cuts, color, styling, or anything you can do with or for hair.

So how do you find out who needs hair models?

One way is to go to **www.Craigslist.com.** Go to the category, "Beauty." In the search box, fill in the word "model." A lot of listings will pop up from stylists or salons that need hair models. It could be from someone who's taking a class, or it could be from an experienced stylist who is moving to a new salon. Sometimes, there might be a nominal cost of $15 or $25 as a product fee if they are doing color – but often, it will be absolutely free!

The ads usually tell you if they need someone for a specific kind of service. This might include whether they will do your color, or highlights, or need to cut long hair to a bob, or a layered cut, or if they are doing a Brazilian blowout or just a blow dry. As I'm typing this, I just got an offer from an ad I answered for a free blow dry just two blocks from me this afternoon! So, tonight, I am going to look bee-yoo-ti-ful!

Hair model opportunities are also available at **www.SalonApprentice.com**. You sign up for free and get 75 to 100 percent off salon prices. Salon Apprentice operates in many big cities, including New York, Chicago, Los Angeles, San Francisco, Las Vegas, Atlanta, Austin, Minneapolis, Denver, Miami, Seattle, St. Louis, Washington DC, Dallas, and more. Check to see if they are in your city.

Another way to become a hair model: check with some of the **salons in your area**. Some high end salons hold classes for their assistants, or for new employees or students who will be practicing in their salon. Again, you may get an appointment for free or, if you are getting color, it may cost $25 to $35 to get color and a blow dry. The students are always supervised by more experienced stylists, who make sure it is done right. Keep in mind, if it's being done by a student, it may take a little longer than usual. But sometimes, you may end up with a fabulous hairdo at less than 1/3 of the price . . . or totally free. The truth is, just because you pay primo prices for a haircut doesn't mean that you are going to love it.

"Some of the worst mistakes in my life were haircuts."
–Jim Morrison

Love Is in the Hair

The fact is, you can go to a high-priced salon and get a cut that you *hate*. Or you can get a fantastic cut that is discounted or free. It's not always about the price. It's about whether or not the stylist is "gifted." Sometimes, someone new can have a special skill or talent, while someone at a fancy salon may not be as good, or might just be having a bad day. Only, in this case it's *your* Bad Hair Day! One of my friends went for a haircut and color in Beverly Hills at a super fancy salon, and her stylist "neglected her." He went out to get lunch, and his coworkers couldn't find him. Twenty minutes later, her hair ended up *stark white and fried!* And she was paying $250 for the privilege of being at an elite salon.

As for me, I figure I'd rather NOT pay and be unhappy than PAY and be *un*happy. (That's how I feel about singles dances, too. I refuse to go to them. Why should I *pay money* to NOT meet someone, when I can *NOT pay* to NOT meet someone!) Of course, whether it's meeting a new date or getting a new haircut, I'd rather be happy with the result. The bottom line is: you may be able to get fabulous results with low prices, too.

I've been a hair model tons of times, and saved thousands of dollars. Sometimes for a cut; sometimes highlights; sometimes getting my roots colored. Did my hair turn pink? Blue? Striped? No. Like with anything, sometimes I *loved* the results. Sometimes, I didn't. But guess what! My hair always grew back. And, lucky for me, it grows back fast. But the point is, it cost very little, or was totally FREE! Because I answered an ad on Craigslist to be a hair model. If I had gone to these salons as a regular client, it probably would have cost $200 to $300 for the exact same services. So, check out Craigslist under "Beauty," Salonapprentice.com, or call and ask the salons in your area if they need hair models.

Here are some salons in Los Angeles that have programs where they use hair models: Carlton, Studio DNA; Joseph Martin; Louis Lacardi, Forme, Nelson J, and many others.

> "There's a reason why forty, fifty, and sixty don't look the way they used to, and it's not because of feminism, or better living through exercise. It's because of hair dye. In the 1950's, only 7 percent of American women dyed their hair; today, there are parts of Manhattan and Los Angeles where there are no gray-haired women at all." –Nora Ephron

My Most Unusual Hair Model Story

I have been a hair model for all kinds of salons, for all kinds of services: cuts, color, Keratin, highlights, bayalage, you name it. The most unusual experience was at Point De Vue. They were looking for a model with grey roots that needed covering – the timing was right, and I answered the ad. I was to be there at 4 p.m., and allot enough time up until 7 p.m.

When I got there, it turned out to be a super-upscale salon where many celebrities go. The owner of the salon was Monica Montoya – who gets over $200 per haircut.

Why did they need models? Their salon had been chosen to be one of the few salons in the country to carry a new color product from

L'Oreal that was now being brought to the U.S. So all their stylists had to become familiar with it. There were two models the day I was there, me and one other, Sheri, who was a Nashville country singer and composer. She had called that morning from a Craigslist ad; I had called the day before.

The salon was beautiful. They offered us café lattes while we waited, and showed us books with all the press they had received in magazines like Allure, Elle, and Vanity Fair, along with photos of the many celebrities who were their clients, including Sharon Stone, Britney Spears, and Jessica Alba. Hey, if it was good enough for them, it was good enough for me!

The five stylists were briefed on the new color techniques, and then both Sheri and I were worked on, by all five of them! Each took different quadrants of our hair and applied the color. Afterwards, we were shampooed and styled.

Voila! – the color was grand, and my hair was absolutely silky smooth. And yes, it made me feel like royalty, being worked on by all these professional stylists! I was living like a millionaire for sure. The cost – ZERO! Hmmm, now if I can just find five *masseuse*s to work on me all at once. Now THAT would be heaven!

Beauty School Drop-In

Another way to save money on your hair is **Beauty Schools.**

In various cities, *Sassoon* has training schools where you can go and get a haircut very inexpensively. Other places in Los Angeles are the *Aveda Institute* and *Hair Art and Science*. There's also *Toni and Guy Hairdressing Academy* in Santa Monica. I have been there numerous times and got a terrific haircut; it's a spacious place with really nice people. I didn't even know about them until I bought a Groupon for two blowdrys for $15! But even without the Groupon, it's extremely economical. Check your city for beauty schools, and also the regular salons that have training programs.

And for beauty, we're not talking just "hair" – I recently saw an ad for free spray tanning by a professional. Again, she was "auditioning" for a new tanning salon, and needed some models to show them what she could do. And then there are manicures and massages.

Rub Me the Right Way

> "I want somebody to give me a great $30 massage, as opposed to a bad $265 massage." –Josh Brolin

One of my true pleasures in life is getting a **massage or facial**. I would love to do it more often, but most of the time I'm too busy writing to take time off and relax. Not to mention, massages and facials can be extremely costly. Especially if you have them at a fancy spa! Let's start with some places big celebs and real millionaires might frequent. At the Hotel Bel-Air Spa by La Prairie, a *White Caviar Illuminating Facial* costs $1,000. OMG, I don't know about you, but I don't have a major urge to have someone rub fish eggs over my face for a cool thou. Or even for a lot less! Hey, I could always buy a can of sardines and just smoosh it across my cheeks, and it would cost about seventy-nine cents (for the can at Ralph's Supermarket.) Other facials there cost as "little" as $270, or even $210; and an hour-long Swedish massage, which is my favorite thing in the world, is priced at $190. Of course, that doesn't include the tip, which at a place like Hotel Bel-Air should be substantial. At the Spa at the Four Seasons

Westlake Village, you can get space-agey facials from Anti-Gravity for $250 to $2,000! So, even at deluxe hotel spas, there is a wide spread of services and prices. But all higher than I can afford. But then, you say, at these beautiful hotels, you also get ritzy, luxurious environments . . . and maybe see Hollywood stars, right?

I don't blame you for wanting to be surrounded by the ultra-lavish furnishings and sumptuous environments. But did you know, if you want to enjoy those ultra-lavish furnishings and environment and see all the wealthy peeps and possibly Hollywood stars, you can just go and hang out in their lobby . . . for free?! Then, go take yourself to a less expensive, but still completely relaxing and wonderful massage or facial – for so many dollars less!

There are other so-called luxury day spas, like the popular Burke-Williams, that are less than the uber-elite hotels, where a one-hour massage might be only $119. Not so bad, you say.

Yet, there are other considerably cheaper options that can give you the same feeling of relaxation and luxury. Some membership spas have been popping up around town, like Massage Envy – where they charge you a yearly membership fee, for which you get a massage every month – and any extra massages are provided at a discounted rate. Numerous other massage places offer $40/hour massages. You'll also find some Asian spas, like one near my home, that gives a marvelous combination hour-long foot and body massage for $39. I have even seen quite a few Japanese foot massage parlors that offer foot massages, along with shoulders and back, for a mere $19 per hour. And I'm NOT talking about the places that give "happy endings." I don't know *those* places and, personally, wouldn't go to them.

Again, just because you go to an expensive spa, doesn't mean you will find someone who is "gifted" and has "the touch" you like. Some masseuses are talented; some have a "tableside" manner that you like; and some don't. I just prefer to enjoy someone who is gifted at massage . . . but not at emptying my wallet.

Mani, Pedi, Hapi Me

Another necessity for me is getting my nails done. This is definitely not a luxury – having beautiful nails makes me look good and feel feminine. The problem is my nails grow very fast and I have to get them done at least every three weeks. I've tried going without my visit to the nail salon, and always realize within days, I simply can't give it up. It turns out when I try to do my own nails, I'm spastic; holding a tiny brush and staying between the lines is foreign to me.

> **"No one likes getting their nails done more than I do."**
> **–Serena Williams**

And, speaking of foreign: again, I choose to go Asian. For manicures and pedicures, you can go to a fancy nail salon and pay premium prices, or you can go to a Vietnamese nail salon. These have sprung up all over in most cities, and they are quite economical. The Vietnamese shops charge a fraction of what the fancier salons charge . . . and I don't think you'll find much difference in how your nails look when you leave. What's the difference? For sure, the atmosphere.

What Happens at the *Nail Salon* . . . Stays at the *Nail Salon*

Oftentimes, the Vietnamese shopkeepers will speak in their own language. A big joke about these places seems to be that they are talking about . . . YOU! Whether or not this is true . . . just sit back and enjoy a manicure or pedicure for $10 to $25; whereas, at a regular salon, it might cost you $40 to $60. Not only that, but whenever I go for a fill and/or pedicure at my nail salon, I have a male manicurist, Tom, who I adore, and he gives the very best shoulder and back massages I have *ever* had! So much so, I often go to him just for a massage. They have a room in the back where I can get a full body massage for just $40. Compare that to the $200 massage I would get at a hotel, and he is just a few blocks away where I can pop in at any time. What's more, if I just want a quickie – a quickie massage, that is – I can stop by for a 15-minute or half hour massage for $10 or $20.

If you want some laughs, I recommend you check out this hilarious animated YouTube video about nail salons: **https://www.youtube.com/watch?v=92fD8Cy2zL0**

One day, when I get my reality show, I will have an episode called "The Massage Competition." I'll set up massage chairs in the street. Passersby will sit down. Then, I'll have three different massage therapists give them fifteen minutes each. Let's see WHICH therapist they choose . . . the $300 masseur; the $150 masseuse; or Tom, my Vietnamese manicurist who charges $40 an hour! He has the best touch in town!

> "I love a massage. I'd go every day if I could. I don't need to be wrapped in herbs like a salmon fillet, but I do love a massage." –Jason Bateman

Something's Afoot!

Not to detract from my super-duper nailmeister Tom and his gifted touch when it comes to massage – the environment of his particular salon isn't the best. If I want a more relaxing, quieter atmosphere, but still a really inexpensive massage, I'll head over to one of the numerous foot spas in the area. My girlfriend Deborah recently told me about one that offers an hour foot massage for $25. They also offer a one hour whole body massage for $45. But, she cautioned me, "Don't spend the $45, because even when you get the $25 foot massage, they are going to do your whole body!"

I went one afternoon, and she was right on the money, i.e. saving me $20! That's because, in addition to doing foot reflexology, they included a good 20 minutes or more massaging my legs, arms, shoulders, back and neck. There was relaxing music playing in a quiet, calm environment, without the chatty background voices I often hear when I get my foot or back rubs at my nail salon.

There are quite a few other Asian foot spas in different areas near my home, and many advertise their services for $25 an hour. One I go to is $39/hr which includes a 20-minute foot massage first, followed by a 40-minute all-body massage. So check around to find a place near you and see what they offer and what they charge.

It's SPActacular!

There are lots of wonderful and luxurious spas throughout the country where you can go for a week or weekend getaway. The prices range from economical to exorbitant, depending upon the specific resort. Groupon and Living Social often have deals on spas and resorts. You can get great discounts on these, and there are even ways to get a weekend at a spa for *free*. Check out the "Getaways and Globetrotting Galore" and "Giving, Getting, and Gala-vanting" chapters to find out how I did it, and how you can, too!

"Hello, Gorgeous!" –Barbra Streisand in Funny Girl

A Wake-Up About Makeup

I buy cosmetics from two places: department stores, and drugstores. Macy's, Nordstrom, Bloomingdale's, Saks – they all have a wonderful assortment of different cosmetic brands with beauty consultants right there to help you select what you need. However, the only time I buy makeup is when they have a "gift with purchase." At least, that way, I feel like I'm getting something extra with my retail purchase. I happen to like Lancôme and Estee Lauder. But most of the companies have promotions at least twice a year or more. So I wait till I can get a great new cosmetic bag or tote bag filled with other beauty products from the brand. This means I never "buy" mascara, because it always seems like mascara is included in these gifts. Often there are lipsticks, too, but not usually the colors I like.

"The best thing is to look natural, but it takes makeup to look natural." –Calvin Klein

In any case, I wait till they have a promotion, and then stock up on the products I like from the brand – and get my additional gifts. Some of these gifts are fabulous. They are often pretty cosmetic bags or tote bags filled with different beauty products. Some of these will be things you don't or *won't* use. Instead of keeping the items you don't use, have a makeup party with girlfriends, and trade them for the things you like from what the other gals bring. Or you can give your unwanted products as gifts; I like to fill up little baskets with an assortment of different items and give them as gifts for holidays or birthdays, or when I go to visit a friend, just as a little surprise. Your friends will love you for this. And you'll all look more beautiful, too!

> **"Honey, I am going to my grave with my eyelashes and my makeup on." –Tammy Faye Bakker**

Another thing to note about department store brands is that you can get your makeup done there. When I was going to have some photos taken, I made an appointment at one of the department store cosmetic counters, and they did my makeup for FREE! You may want to buy something while you're there, but it's not an absolute necessity. Just say you'll come back another time. (Especially if there's a promotion coming up!)

Drugstore makeup can often be just as good as more expensive brands – in fact, some of their brands are made by the same companies! They are just marketed differently. When you're out at a party, someone may notice if you are wearing Manolo Blahnik heels, but no one will know if you have powdered your face with Mac or L'Oreal or Neutrogena. Just get a product that you feel good in, and that makes you feel good . . . but doesn't make your wallet feel bad!

> **"The only way I'd be caught without makeup is if my radio fell in the bathtub while I was taking a bath and electrocuted me and I was in between makeup at home. I hope my husband would slap a little lipstick on me before he took me to the morgue." –Dolly Parton**

Look DIVINE by Going ONLINE

Also, if you shop a certain brand, they can often be found online at serious discounts.

Online Sites that have beauty products include **www.Groupon.com** and **www.LivingSocial.com**, as well as others like **www.Overstock.com and www.eBay.com**. Also, you can just Google your favorite brand, or as I like to say, "Google for discounts." Comparison shop! If you're looking for a name brand on something, chances are you can get it at a discount, and that can be waaaay below the retail price.

On the day I checked the health and beauty section at Overstock.com, they had designer perfumes from Versace, Dolce and Gabana, Gucci, Calvin Klein, and Polo, to name just a few, for up to 71 percent off the retail price. Not to mention cosmetics and hair wands, body groomers, shavers, mirrors, and anything and everything at tremendous savings.

www.Temptalia.com is a niche site for cosmetics that offers a database of over 75,000 known dupes to help you find an alternative to the product you had your eye on – whether it's for something cheaper, by another brand, or available when you couldn't find yours.

Buy. Try. Apply.

Beauty bloggers and vloggers are another way to find bargains or even free giveaways. You can get awesome tips on not only *where* to buy it, but *how* to apply it! YouTube has made gazillions for numerous beauty gurus telling their fans all kinds of ways to look sensational. Michelle Phan, Lisa Eldridge, and Zoella are three who have become household names from their useful and fun makeup tutorials.

Life of the Partay

Another way to get free makeup is to hold a **beauty party.** Lots of in-home makeup consultants will give you complimentary products if you invite friends and have a party. They'll have fun and get discounts, and you might end up with a cache of cool cosmetics.

Instead of Tupperware parties, these are cosmetic parties. Not only can you buy makeup, you can possibly even make some cash for yourself by shopping with a makeup carrier that sells through consultants. A girlfriend of mine is an Arbonne consultant. She has frequent parties to introduce people to her products. She also makes lots of money herself – as well as getting sensational trips and bonuses. In just the past year, she's been on free trips to New York, Las Vegas and Hawaii . . . as well as an all-expense paid cruise with her lucky hubby. In fact, her husband, who is a Hollywood writer, liked all the perks and money so much that he became an Arbonne rep, too – and is now selling their men's line to all *his* friends in *show biz.*

Companies like Arbonne and Mary Kay Cosmetics offer private in-home makeup parties and create income for their consultants as well as giving them a lifestyle that enables them to work at home and make friends while they earn a living. It may not be for you, but it's certainly worth going to an event to see what they are about and enjoying the perks of the party.

Beauty supply shops can be good places to find all kinds of cosmetics and paraphernalia, just make sure you are not paying more than usual, and hopefully less. Or you can check out the brands you like and then shop online for the best deals.

There are also many **"freebie" sites online** that offer lots of complimentary samples, such as **www.freebies.com**. Usually, with these sites, you end up getting lots of emails as well, so I recommend you use an email address that's dedicated to offers and promotions.

HEALTHY, Not WEALTHY, but WISE!

> "Everybody gets sick; everybody has had a problem with insurance or the prescription drugs they're supposed to be taking or an elderly parent who needs care." –Michael Moore

Yes, there are some times when you can utilize health services "like you're a millionaire," as well. Most chiropractors will give you your first visit free. And sometimes with it, a massage! Dentists often need a patient to pass their board exams on. They may be new dentists, but not necessarily. We all know that the cost of medical services in the United States can be astronomical, which is why some people even choose to go abroad where the services are substantially less expensive. There are many options; here are some of my experiences and some other things I've heard about but, luckily, being generally healthy, never had to consider.

Nothing But the Tooth!

I moved to Los Angeles from New York. I had been here several years when I got a call from my New York City dentist who I had really liked a lot. He was moving to Los Angeles so, although he had been in practice for twenty years as a dentist, in order to pass his California boards, he needed to bring in a patient to work on. He asked me; I said yes; and he did *all my dental work for free*, using the session to pass his California Boards. Now he has a thriving practice in Woodland Hills. I thought I should get a percentage of his practice, because he ultimately got it because he used my teeth to pass his boards! Of course, it didn't exactly work out that way – but I did get my initial dentistry here from him.

Now that dentists and doctors can advertise, they often send out special offers in Valpak or coupon pamphlets and some are even on sites like Groupon and Living Social. Wherever you find them, before you go, please check them out online. Sites like Yelp and others have lots of reviews and reading them can give you an idea of what other people's experiences have been with specific dentists.

There are also dental schools all over the U.S. and they often have programs where people can get dental care of all kinds. Students are always supervised by experienced dentists, so it may work out fine to go there for your general dental needs. Again, I would recommend checking to see what the reviews are on the school or the dental care they provide.

There are also, of course, numerous dental insurance programs, like Delta Dental and others. Just check them out to make sure they cover the kinds of services you might need.

> **"To keep the body in good health is a duty . . . otherwise we shall not be able to keep our mind strong and clear." –Buddha**

Don't Go Mental About It!

Frequently, psychologists will give you your first session for free, and oftentimes they will work with you so that if you have insurance, it will be covered by your insurance. Also, many mental health workers have sliding scales so that you pay according to your individual ability. In any case, it is always good to ASK. You lose nothing . . . and you may have a lot to gain. Another way to spend less is to see if your therapist has group therapy available, since that will be less costly. And just think: that way, you can meet a bunch of other wackos who are in much worse shape than you!

> **"I go to group therapy. I'm the only one there, but I have multiple personalities."** –Marilyn Anderson

Nips and Tucks for Way Less Bucks

I live in Los Angeles. Home of Hollywood stars, celebrities, and California surfer girls with long blonde tresses, golden tans and perfect bodies and faces. Now, we all know that many of them didn't start out so perfect – a nip here, a tuck there, and a bit of a bosom boost between! How many women these days haven't had a few surgical adjustments to help them look beautiful and dazzling?

Here I am, a baby boomer – one of the few who has never gotten a nose job, Botox, boob job, lifts, lipo, Lattisse, none of it. I was the original *au naturel* girl. And then one day, a couple of years ago, I started noticing changes. Drooping, sagging, "leaning to the left" changes. OMG. No, I'm not talking about drooping tatas or sagging buttocks. Eeeek – my beak!

When I was 16, all the girls in my school were getting **nose jobs** to straighten out their bumps and make their noses cute and bunny-like. (I'm talking Playboy Bunny, not Easter Bunny.) But not me! I didn't feel the need to have my nose shortened, ski-sloped or *bunnified.* My nose wasn't perfect by any means. It had a little bump, but I was happy with it, and I would brag that I had a Roman nose. It had *character.* It was the real "me."

Cut to: Decades later. I first realized my profile had changed when I was a guest on a television show, and they filmed me from the side. Watching myself that night, I was less interested in my clever and informative repartee . . . than in the way I looked. Yikes! I couldn't believe it. *WHO* is *THAT?*

It didn't look at all like me. It wasn't the nose I'd grown up with . . . or even the nose I'd had a year before. It had drooped, hollowed out and looked bumpy and crooked. I was aghast. I wasn't 16 anymore, but now, I was ready for that nose job – or was I?

I went to an ear, nose and throat specialist to see if it was a medical problem. No, I could breathe fine. However, the doctor told me a "turbinate" had collapsed. To fix it was cosmetic, and of course, *that* would require rhinoplasty.

It was my understanding that rhinoplasty = surgery + pain + recovery time. Not to mention a hefty bill in the thousands! They told me it **could cost from $10,000 to $15,000.** Yikes!

That's when I discovered there is a different kind of nose job. Not the $10,000 to $15,000 go-to-the-hospital, break-your-nose, risk-complications, take-months-to-heal kind of nose job. No, this was a take-out-the-bump-make-your-nose-look-beautiful nose job, but it would cost only about $1,000 to $2,500. Quite a difference!

And even better – the nose isn't broken; there's no cutting, no general anesthesia, and no post op. You are in and out of the doctor's office in less than an hour, and can even go back to work.

The procedure is called the **15-Minute-Nose Job** or the **Non-Surgical Nose Job**. This revolutionary, non-invasive alternative to surgical rhinoplasty was created by Dr. Alexander Rivkin in 2004. More formally known as **Injection Rhinoplasty,** it resolves the appearance of bumps, drooping tips, and crooked noses safely and quickly, without the risks and long, painful recovery normally associated with rhinoplasty surgery. In this procedure, small injections of a cosmetic filler are placed into locations around the nose precisely targeted to change the nose shape in the desired manner.

A few different fillers can be used. Juvederm, Restylane, Perlane, Voluma or Radiesse are injectable fillers that can last from 10 months to two or three years, and Artefill is a permanent filler that lasts forever. Many doctors in different cities currently offer this as an alternative to rhinoplastic surgery.

I *Nose* It's True

I decided THIS was the kind of nose job I wanted. I went to the office for a consultation and was told I would be a perfect candidate. So I scheduled the nose job, went in, and half hour later, was back in my car driving home. Although it was a little swollen at first, it calmed down after a few days, and my nose has looked great ever since!

The night of the procedure my friend Felice came over and said my nose looked "amazing." "Wow, it's better than a real nose job!" she remarked. "I can't believe you just walked in and out." I was delighted Felice gave me 10 stars. She revealed to me that, over the years, she'd had six traditional nose jobs (real surgery and real pain!), so she should *know* what's good. Felice *loves* my doctor and she's never even met him! And her nose jobs cost many thousands more than my 15-minute nose job! As for me, I was super pleased with the results. And I'm not a cosmetic procedures virgin anymore!

I have to confess to you that, although this non-surgical nose job usually costs from $600 to $2,500 depending on the doctor and the city, I did get *my* nose job for free. What, you say? How did I do that? When I got my initial consultation, I ASKED. I told the doctor I wrote articles for various magazines, and respectfully queried him, "If I write about you, can you do the nose job without charging me?" He agreed.

Well, you think, YOU aren't a writer, so how can *you* get a nose job . . . or Botox, or cosmetic injections, or a chin job, new boobs, or whatever . . . without paying a primo price . . . or without paying anything?

Not Spending on Mending

Sometimes, doctors need patients for filming, so they can put the procedure on their website or on YouTube or on a television show. When you visit for your consultation, "ask" if your doctor ever needs patients for filming, and *that question* may get you the discount (or even complimentary procedure) you want.

Sometimes, I've seen listings on Craigslist from medical offices offering patients complimentary services in order to film them or try new procedures. I've even gotten emails from the office where I got my nose job indicating they are offering some free beauty procedures, and to forward the message to anyone who might have interest.

Unhappy Feet? Don't Foot the Bill

In addition, some offices do clinical trials for medical services. I have bunions on my feet, and several times I've been contacted by a medical office offering to operate on my bunions for free as part of a study they were doing. I know it's a difficult surgery that requires a lot of recovery time, so I've always said no. But if it was something I truly needed or wanted, I would consider it. There are always lots of clinical trials for all kinds of medical conditions that go on at different medical companies, and sometimes they will even PAY YOU to take part in these.

> "All the money in the world can't buy you back good health." —Reba McEntire

Of course, the bottom line with any doctors, dentists, or medical personnel is to check and make sure they are reputable physicians with accreditation and a good reputation. Even if it's discounted or "free," you want to be sure, first and foremost, that it is safe and that your doctor is a good one.

Other Ways to Get Medical Procedures

Some of the Groupon and Living Social or other sites have discount offers for cosmetic procedures at medical offices or spas, as do some individual doctor's websites.

I always get coupons in the mail that offer discounts for dental cleanings and X-rays, or on cosmetic procedures from doctors or dentists who want to attract new patients. It's fine to check these out, but please *do some research* to make sure these are reputable places. Do your homework before going to anyone for things as important as your health and well-being. If you get a bad haircut at a salon, your hair will grow back, but when dealing with physicians or dentists, you shouldn't take any chances.

> "At Thanksgiving, I always start at the top of my list and say I'm grateful for friends, family, and good health. Then I get more superficial . . . like being thankful for my Louboutins." –Christie Brinkley

Another example is something my father went through. He had been experiencing difficulty swallowing, and was told he had an esophageal shelf. The doctors he went to said there was NOTHING to be done to fix it. I searched the Internet. Guess what – I found out there was a doctor at a prestigious medical facility in South Carolina doing a procedure that would correct my father's problem. It was just an outpatient procedure, and the doctor had gotten extremely positive results with many patients.

My father's physicians had said there was "nothing that could be done," because THEY didn't do it. So don't just take your current professional's word for it. Whether it's doctors, dentists, cosmetic surgeons, hairdressers, or whoever – if you want to be sure – ask around, and DO THE RESEARCH. People may tell you something isn't available . . . because THEY don't offer it. But these days, there are many ways to find things even when the first, second or third person you ask says it doesn't exist.

Medical Tourism

Another way that lots of people get better pricing on surgeries, whether cosmetic or otherwise, is to go to different countries. Certain countries are known for cosmetic procedures; others have specialties regarding the treatment of different conditions or diseases. If you want to go abroad, there's no doubt you can save many thousands of dollars on all kinds of procedures and surgeries. Here is a chart comparing prices in different countries from MedicalTourism.com.

http://medicaltourism.com/Forms/price-comparison.aspx

Again, PLEASE, make sure you research the facilities, no matter where you go in the U.S. or abroad. But recognize that there are often alternative places overseas, and sometimes they are quite good or even world-renowned. Bottom line, especially when you are dealing with your health and well-being: DO YOUR RESEARCH!

Is the High Price of Prescriptions . . . Making You Sick?

"I believe in prescription drugs. I believe in feeling better." –Denis Leary

I'm a druggie. Not really. But I do have to take some prescription drugs. Let's face it. You almost have to BE A MILLIONAIRE to afford prescriptions these days – and that's even WITH INSURANCE!

So I checked out ways to get my pills – for less. You might have high cholesterol or diabetes, or you might have broken your leg – or you might just be *out of your mind* – and need a pill. Whatever the reason, why should you pay an arm and a leg, or through the nose – or up the wazoo – to treat any part of your body?

A lot of people I know get meds online. Or from Canada, or other countries. Maybe that works. I don't know; I've never tried it. If you're new at buying drugs this way, please make sure you're getting the same exact prescription and that the online store can be trusted.

"I want a schedule-keeping, waking-up-early, wallet-carrying, picture-hanging man. I don't care if he takes prescription drugs for cholesterol or hair loss." –Mindy Kaling

I have personally tried a few other things that truly lower my cost for prescriptions.

For instance, did you know a lot of pharmacies have Prescription Drug Programs where they carry **generic drugs for $4 for a 30-day supply**; or **$10 for a 3-month supply?** These are available to everyone, no membership required. They have over 500 different prescription medicines for different illnesses or conditions at your local pharmacies. Walmart, Target, CVS, Costco, Rite-Aid, even Kroger and Ralph's Supermarkets to name just a few: they all have $4 generic programs.

Go online to these and look at their lists. Or, ask at your local pharmacy. You can also go to **www.MyFourDollarDrugList.com** and put in the name of the drug, and they'll list the pharmacies near you.

But What If It's Not on the $4 Generic List?

For this, I've used **www.GoodRX.com.** This is a site where you get a FREE discount drug card that provides incredible savings on prescriptions, also *at your local pharmacy!* When I used them, I got even better prices than through my insurance.

Sometimes it's 80 percent less than *without the card.* I had a prescription that would have cost me a $120 co-pay with my insurance. With the card, it cost me $32 for a three-month supply. Not bad, huh?

It's free to join online, and then they'll send you a GoodRX discount card. Again, it's for pharmacies in your neighborhood like Walgreens, Target, Rite-Aid, and CVS. GoodRX.com tells you the prices at each pharmacy, with or without your Good Rx card; and, let me tell you, it's usually a huge difference.

There's another site called **www.WellRx.com**, which seems to have a similar set up, although I haven't personally used them. For any of these, the $4 programs or the discount drug cards, you'll need a prescription when you order. But, whether you're a millionaire or not, why pay a fortune for drugs? Instead, spend your money on other *fun* things. Like buying this book! And getting more for friends!

"Happiness is good health and a bad memory." –Ingrid Bergman

In addition, some pharmacies will give additional discounts on the price of prescriptions to various membership organizations, including Triple A and AARP, or even company discounts, depending on where you work. You won't know unless you ASK!

So, don't be a pill! Check them out: the $4 Generic Prescription Programs at lots of pharmacies; **www.MyFourDollarDrugList.com**; **www.GoodRX.com**; and **www.WellRx.com**. You can probably find others as well.

And now, I'll just take a Happy Pill!

Chap Wrap 'n Recap

The Beauty Buzz

- Become a Hair Model
- Groupons, Living Social, Yipit
- Beauty Schools
- Comparison Shop
- Drugstore Cosmetics
- Complimentary Makeup Sessions

The Health Buzz

- $4 Prescription Program
- GoodRx.com
- Medical Procedures Abroad
- Do the Research
- 15-Minute Nose Job Instead of Rhinoplasty

Looking Good! Feeling Good! Quiz – True or False

If I want a new haircut . . .

1. I'll pay big bucks, and it will definitely be gorgeous.
2. To save money, I'll try being a hair model.
3. I can get deals at Yelp.com, Yipit.com and YikesYouScalpedMe.com.

If I need surgery . . .

1. I'll take a trip to Mexico and ask a guy with a donkey where the nearest doc is.

2. I'll let a cosmetic surgeon operate because he says I'll be cuter after I pay him.

3. I'll do research on the doctors who do the procedure and ask for references.

6. Getaways and Globetrotting Galore

"Twenty years from now you will be more disappointed by the things you didn't do than by the ones you did do. So throw off the bowlines, sail away from the safe harbor. Catch the trade winds in your sails. Explore. Dream. Discover." –Mark Twain

Traveling is a passion for me. I love discovering new places, foods and people. But it wasn't always this way. I've gone through different phases.

Decades ago, when I worked a "real" job, I traveled on business. It's always fun going to new places when your company is paying the bill. They put you up at a nice hotel; you get to enjoy great meals at great restaurants; and when it's over, you submit an expense report. I worked at the National Academy of Sciences in Washington DC for several years, and flew to various conferences in different cities, always leaving a little extra time to explore my new surroundings. But after a few years, I realized I wasn't fulfilled, even with all the perks of the job. Science just wasn't my destiny. What was? SHOW BIZ!

So, I left my well-paying scientific public relations job and headed to New York to go into the insecure, never-knows-what's-going-to-happen, probably-won't-ever-make-any-decent-money, will-most-likely-become-a-waitress field of show business.

I wanted to be an ACTRESS! So, there I was, in New York. Not working. Waiting for calls from agents, producers and casting directors. Waiting, waiting, and waiting. I suddenly had loads of time on my hands.

Aha! Not working, I had *more time* to travel, but I didn't want to leave town because I was afraid I'd miss my big break! Little did I know that the best way to get offered a big break is to go away! It's that old adage: Everyone wants you when they can't have you!

I spent several years in the Big Apple, not traveling. Oh, I got a number of acting gigs here and there; but, as you know by now (since you haven't seen me in any movies or TV series) – I didn't become a star.

Then one day, I decided to move to Los Angeles, where my career would take another turn – and I became a writer. Again, I was afraid to leave town because I might miss my big break.

During the last twenty years in Los Angeles, I've actually traveled more than ever. I've stopped worrying about that big break; I think I missed it! However, by now, I had no company paying my way, and didn't have enough money to do the kind of traveling I wanted. Instead, I became resourceful. And that's what I'm going to share with you. As a not-a-millionaire-but-lives-like-one, I've found many ways to enjoy luxury adventures, and now my secrets are going to become your secrets, too.

> **"The cool thing about being famous is traveling. I have always wanted to travel across seas, like to Canada and stuff." –Britney Spears**

It's All Relative

You have to visit your relatives . . . even if you don't like them!

My parents and my ex-boyfriend's mom lived in South Florida, so we spent a lot of time going back and forth across the country from Los Angeles to Boca Raton, FL, to visit them.

He liked to travel by car, and wanted me to accompany him. I hate driving on freeways (I'm a nervous passenger), so I told him I'd go by car, but only if we could take regular roads, make lots of stops, and turn it into a vacation. In addition, since I'd just published my first book, I'd be able to do book signings or events along the way, as well as appear on local radio or TV shows. My boyfriend agreed, and we decided to take our first trip that would last three weeks. We ended up going back and forth this way four times, and always had a blast. Why? Because we visited interesting attractions, met wonderful people, and stayed at fantastic places.

He wasn't working, and neither was I. So how did we do it? I knew we could go on our own nickel, so to speak, and stay at Motel 6s or Best Westerns, and eat at local diners and coffee shops. Or, we could stay at four or five-star hotels and get exceptional meals at high-class restaurants . . . and not have to pay hardly anything! Duh, which would YOU choose?

I decided to call a few hotels to see if they would "host" us, by telling them I was a travel reporter and would write an article about their hotel. Btw, I had told a number of travel reporters I was going to do this, and they all insisted that unless I was a seasoned journalist who worked for a big magazine like *Conde Nast*, or a newspaper like *The New York Times*, no hotels or restaurants would ever comp me. They told me over and over: "It's impossible." "It'll never happen." "You can't do it." "No way!"

It's a good thing I didn't listen to those naysayers. For over five years, my boyfriend and I traveled all across the U.S., staying in fabulous hotels and getting phenomenal meals . . . and most of them were totally complimentary.

> **"I have found out that there ain't no surer way to find out whether you like people or hate them than to travel with them."** –Mark Twain

Travel Reporting Can Be Fun

Now, keep in mind, I *did* write the articles. I found several online magazines that wanted travel articles; they didn't pay reporters, but willingly accepted articles from them. I created my own travel section in *Agenda Magazine* and called it "Romance on the Road." I titled it that, because I didn't want "bargain" travel or "family" travel. I wanted "luxury" travel.

Some of the places I stayed at included the honeymoon suite at the Monterey Hotel and Spa, with dinner and lunch in their restaurants, and a couples massage. We spent several nights in the Ernest Hemingway Suite at the Hotel Monteleone in New Orleans, and practically had our own swimming pool right outside our door on the rooftop. We vacationed at a magnificent plantation in Monmouth, Virginia, and in a sprawling condo suite in St. George, Utah. Then, I was invited for a five-star, all-expenses paid trip to Taiwan, visiting many different cities there by bus, train and plane. That was a press junket with 14 other reporters.

The point is: I never planned any of this. It just sort of "happened," because I wanted to travel and didn't have any money. So I used my creativity to "create" a possibility. It ended up being an exciting and glorious five years.

> **"People don't take trips . . . trips take people."**
> –John Steinbeck

So How Can YOU Be a Travel Reporter?

Start writing. Every time you go on a trip, write up the hotel, the restaurants, and the attractions. You can start your own blog. Or write up the places you stay at on Trip Advisor or Yelp, keeping all your reviews in a file. Then, if you approach a magazine or newspaper, you'll have "clips" (which means the articles or blurbs) to show their editors.

Keep in mind: *you don't have to travel* to be a *travel reporter*. You can start by writing about places in your own city, whether it's restaurants, hotels, or attractions. The thing is to get started. Practice writing a few paragraphs about places you like. There are so many online sites that need content, so if you write interesting articles, especially on unique places in your neighborhood, you can submit them and, if accepted, you'll be "published." Soon you'll have a portfolio of clips you can send out to places when you want to get comped as a travel writer.

Also, make yourself a business card that says Travel Reporter. When you go out, whether it's to restaurants, attractions or hotels, give your cards out. You may also want to have a website where you post your articles or blurbs.

Travel reporters who write for traditional newspapers or magazines get paid for their articles. Although I wrote numerous pieces for which I was compensated, I was happy to contribute to online magazines where I didn't get paid but where my accommodations and meals were my perks. The reason I often preferred it was that this way, I didn't have to pitch ideas and "hope" I'd get an assignment. More importantly, I didn't have to adhere to strict deadlines that would put me under a lot of pressure. I arranged the trips myself and then submitted them, so I wouldn't have to deal with a publisher or editor telling me what to write, or asking me to do rewrites, or demanding it be done by a certain time.

Check out magazines or newspapers to see if they have submission policies. You can also Google "travel writing" or "travel reporter jobs," or just go to the myriad of websites online and see where the kinds of articles you might want to write are being posted. Then, see who you can contact there to pitch ideas or make submissions.

If you're arranging things yourself (after you've got a portfolio), you can contact a city's visitor and convention center. On their website, it usually indicates a "press" or "media" section. Click on it, and you'll find contact information for their public relations office. The nice thing about going through the visitor's center or PR people is that they will often plan the itinerary for you and arrange your hotels, restaurants, and attractions. It's less work for you, and they know which hotels and restaurants are available and want press coverage.

You can also contact hotels on your own. But don't ask for the desk clerk! Again, you'll want to find the public relations people or, with smaller venues, the manager or owner of the establishment. Just remember, before you do this, make sure you have some credibility. No one is going to comp you if you can't prove you'll be of value to them with a published article. As I mentioned above, when I started, I was told no one would comp me, but I had a track record by having published a book, even though it wasn't a book on traveling.

Insider Tip

> If you can write about some aspect of weddings, a lot of high class opportunities can present themselves. Wedding venues love to get coverage. Usually they are upscale places that have wonderful accommodations and amenities.

Some websites that cater to travel reporters include:

www.travmedia.com

www.mediakitty.com

Another possibility is if you're a good photographer. Some of the people I met on my press junket to Taiwan were not writers at all, but were spending their lives traveling the world and taking pictures. So that's another possibility – not just for free travel, but for getting paid for a skill or hobby of yours.

Blogging and Vlogging

Many people are becoming bloggers these days, whether it's to write about travel or another favorite pastime or subject. If you get enough followers, you can get offered amazing opportunities, be it hotels, restaurants, trips, or products like jewelry, watches or apparel, whatever you blog about. I knew a young man who loved watches; he started writing about them on a blog, and now all kinds of watch companies send him their newest styles to review. Even extremely expensive ones!

Find something you are passionate about and start writing about it. You might report on spas or about cuisine, wine, clothing, or about exotic places all over the globe. Start simple, then expand your area. You can use social networking to get an audience and, once you have a track record, you can contact people anywhere in the world to be featured in your blog. You can even get "guest bloggers" to do the writing for you!

In addition, local cable companies have "cable access" shows. Maybe you can create one. Then, when you travel, you can tell hotel or restaurant owners you will feature them on your show.

You can also start a YouTube channel and host your own show there. YouTube has become a major arena for individuals who have started their own shows or channels . . . and become millionaires! And basically, they are just talking about things they love.

So it's true – you can blog or vlog your way to free trips, merchandise, and more!

Check out some of the YouTubers who have become famous and RICH, like Bethany Mota, Glozelle Green, PewDiePie, and Hannah Hart from *My Drunk Kitchen*. Hannah liked to cook, and she liked to drink. So she started filming herself cooking and swilling booze. Now, she not only has a YouTube show, but books, sponsors, fame, and enough money so she doesn't need this book. Even though she'll definitely want one!

But wait, you say, "I'm not a writer. I can't film myself, and I don't drink and cook."

No problem. Don't worry if you're not a whiz of a wordsmith, or outgoing enough to start your own YouTube channel. You don't have to be a writer or YouTuber to travel well without funds, as the following examples will show.

Wrap your Brain around a Free Week in Spain

Would you like to stay for six days at a four-star resort in Spain for FREE? What, you ask? Where? How? *Vaughan Town* is a unique cultural experience that offers English speaking people a chance to have an exciting week at one of four resorts outside of Madrid for FREE by VOLUNTEERING for their program.

VOLUNTEERING? "What does that mean? Do I have to scrub floors? Wash dishes? Be an entertainer?" Nope. All you have to do is speak English and have it be your native language.

The programs are designed for Spanish business people who want to improve their English so they go to one of the resorts for six days and get to chat and share activities with English speaking people – that's YOU, having regular conversations during breakfast, lunch, dinner, and all kinds of activities.

"Wait a minute," you say. "Does that mean I have to be an English teacher?" No. They get all kinds of volunteers: writers, social workers, backpackers, doctors, musicians, students, whatever – ages 18 to 80!

There are four resorts that the programs are held at:

1) Puerta de Gredos in Avila.

2) Hotel de la Villa in Pedraza,

3) El Rancho de la Aldeguela in Segovia

4) Campus Puente Nuevo in Avila.

I'm not sure I can pronounce them right, but they sure seem inviting!

Vaughan Town is a cultural experience that goes on all year long. In each group, you meet around 15 Spaniards and 15 other English speakers and you spend your days in conversations, with funny skits, theater, games and outdoor activities. It's a way to get to know Spanish people and culture first-hand.

You're probably wondering, "How can they do this without me having to pay? Is there a catch?" Nope. Their Spanish clients from big companies pay to attend the program.

Now remember, Vaughan Town is a VOLUNTEER program, which means you'll be volunteering your time to speak English for six days both in groups and one-to-one. This doesn't mean you just talk; it means you'll be sharing your life stories and experiences.

And the people you're with will have different life styles and be from different backgrounds, not just from Spain, but from other English speaking countries like England, Ireland, Australia, New Zealand, South Africa, etc. You can make friends with people from all over the globe. And you just have to speak English.

The only expense is your flights getting to and from Madrid. I suggest you use your frequent flyer miles or try to find a super cheap fare. Or you can put this *volunteer week* at the end or beginning of another trip to Europe.

"Uh-oh," you say, "There's only one problem. I don't speak Spanish." *No problemo.* You don't have to speak Spanish; in fact, you're NOT ALLOWED to speak Spanish.

Their Spanish participants are there to LEARN conversational English. So no speaking Spanish at all!

As long as you speak English, it doesn't matter what your accent is. It can be British, "Cheerio, luv!" Or New York-ese, "Hey, how ya doin', bro?" or Southern, "Ahhhhm just soooo pleased to make your acquaintance, suh!"

You can apply and get more information at their website:

http://volunteers.grupovaughan.com/

I had told my girlfriend, Felice, about Vaughan Town last year. She went last month and had an absolutely AMAZING time. She said it's the best vacation she's ever been on, and that some of the people she met there have been there 15 times!

I had planned to go a couple of years ago with my ex, but he decided he didn't want to, so I didn't go, either. But since Felice told me how much she loved it, I may get around to it soon.

I heard there is a similar program that does this in Turkey, but I don't know anyone who has been there:

http://www.eecanglo.com/en/ or email info@eecanglo.

It's Your BIRTHRIGHT

Birthright Israel, or simply Birthright, is a not-for-profit educational organization that sponsors free ten-day heritage trips to Israel for Jewish young adults, aged 18 to 26. During their trip, participants, most of whom are visiting Israel for the first time, are encouraged to discover new meaning in their personal Jewish identity and connection to Jewish history and culture. Since trips began in the winter of 1999, more than 400,000 young people from 64 countries have participated in the program.

Several travel companies offer deals or discounts to provide similar kinds of trips for adults over 26, especially for the baby boomer generation, over 50 or 60 years old.

Honeymoon Israel is similar to Birthright, but for married couples, especially those in interfaith marriages where one partner is Jewish. Two friends of mine were chosen to be part of it in 2016. There is some payment required, but at a tremendous reduction, and couples get a chance for an incredible honeymoon . . . whether they be newlyweds or those who have been married for years.

> **www.BirthrightIsrael.com**
>
> **www.HoneymoonIsrael.org**

Birthright Israel has inspired similar programs in other countries. **Birthright Armenia, ReConnect Hungary,** and **Birthright Greece** all offer programs for young adults to visit their ancestors' homeland and learn about their culture and heritage.

Volunteer Far and Near

There are many options available for volunteer vacations in other countries and the USA. Depending on the organization involved, there are various terms which generally mean the same thing. You can google phrases such as volunteer vacations, voluntourism, service vacations, international volunteering, volunteer travel, working vacations, gap year travel, volunteer travel, and volunteering abroad or in the U.S.

Some of these are free, some may involve small costs, but all offer the opportunity to see new places and experience different cultures while giving to the community. You might be helping to build houses, hiking and restoring trails, working on a farm, harvesting food, taking care of animals, or just speaking English.

There is a world of possibilities whether you are an individual or a family. Parents with children often like the opportunity to work on a farm, and there are programs both in the U.S. and abroad. As for me, I don't want to milk any cows on my vacation! Spending a week at a beautiful resort and spending my days talking to people is much more my style.

Whatever your style, and whether you're a senior citizen or a college student, a millennial or a baby boomer, remember that just as exciting as exploring new places and meeting new people, is the opportunity to be "giving" to the communities where you volunteer. It makes you *feel rich* when you give to others.

Some examples of organizations that seek volunteers for meaningful trips are:

www.globeaware.org – Offers volunteer vacations in Peru, Costa Rica, Vietnam, Cambodia, Laos, Thailand, Nepal and Brazil.

www.habitat.org – Habitat for Humanity offers opportunities for people to help build homes in different areas of the country or, through their Global Village trips, volunteers can work in more than 40 nations around the world.

www.lead-adventures.com –Volunteer and adventure programs in Ecuador and the Galapagos Islands.

www.Oceanic-Society.org – Offers volunteer and family vacations that focus on protecting marine wildlife and the marine environment through conservation-based research and environmental education in

Central and South America and the Pacific Ocean region.

www.worldteach.org – Year-long and summer programs where volunteers can share their skills and knowledge with people in developing nations in Asia, Africa, the Pacific Islands, Latin America, South America, and the Caribbean.

www.wwoof.net – Opportunities on organic farms in various countries. Volunteers live with their hosts, help with the daily tasks, and experience the life of a farmer.

> **"Bizarre travel plans are dancing lessons from God." –**
> **Kurt Vonnegut**

Okay, so maybe you're not up for a volunteer vacay. Fear not, there are other ways to enjoy travel without spending a bundle.

Swapping, Surfing and Staying for No Cost or Low Cost

I'll stay in yours, if you stay in mine.

It's been around forever, but ever since the 2006 movie, *The Holiday*, starring Cameron Diaz and Kate Winslet, house-swapping has become more well-known. The concept is simple: you swap houses with someone in another city, state, or country. You both get vacations without the high cost of accommodations. It can be for a few days, a few months, or even a year. There are a number of different sites that offer to find house-swapping opportunities for you. My aunt and uncle did this years ago with a family from England. Finally, after a number of years of swapping, they decided to meet each other's families and take a vacation together!

Homeswapping websites:

www.homeexchange.com

www.lovehomeswap.com

www.homelink-usa.org

Couch Potatoes and Home-Bodies

Couchsurfing is another free way to go, although I doubt "millionaires" would do it. You stay for free at someone's house, possibly on a couch, in a room, or in a bed. The value here is that not only is it free, but you get to know the people of a different area and can make great friends. I know some people who have couchsurfed for years, staying at different homes every day, week and month, and they never had to have a home base or pay rent!

You can check it out at **www.couchsurfing.com** or on Twitter @couchsurfing. There are even Couchsurfing Travel Apps on Google Play and iTunes:

Similar to couchsurfing, but not free, and probably a bit more upscale, is the **"home stay."** Homestays allow guests to book a room in a local person's home on a nightly, weekly, or monthly basis for a fee. In all of the homestays, there is a host present during the stay, enhancing the guest's travel experience through their hospitality and local knowledge.

SITES:

www.homestay.com

www.homeaway.com

www.vrbo.com

Air BnB

AirBnB has become well known as an alternative to expensive hotels. You can rent an apartment for a night, a castle for a week, or a villa for a month. The site connects people to unique travel accommodations at any price point in over 34,000 cities and 190 countries. In the U.S., lots of people are jumping at these opportunities. It's not just people who own their homes, but renters who will "move into a friend's or mom's place" for a week or month – so they can rent *their* apartments out to vacationers. These can be excellent possibilities, especially in big cities where hotels are ultra-expensive, and you may be staying for more than just a few days.

Just make sure it's legit, and in an area where you want to be, and as nice as you want it to be! There are all levels of places, some beautiful, some fair, and some probably *almost awful!* Do your research and investigate as much as you can – before you stay . . . and before you pay!

You can even make money renting *your* home out this way. Often you make more money renting a property for a week at a time or a day at a time, than if you do it by the month as an income property. Better still, if you can come up with idea like this, you can probably become a multi-millionaire. The San Francisco based company Air BnB was founded in August 2008, and in 2015 had a valuation of about $20 billion! I only wish I had thought of it!

SITE: www.AirBnB.com

Breakfast in Bed, and Happy Hour, Too

As for me, when I go away, I don't want to have to make beds, cook food, do dishes, or clean up. (Actually, I don't like doing that when

I'm at home, either!) I love having maid service and fresh towels every day (and so far, I haven't found a live-in boyfriend who will do all that!)

On my many treks hither and thither, and as a travel reporter, I have found my favorite stays have been at bed and breakfasts, aka B&Bs. There are all levels of B&Bs, but there's a reason I like them, especially the luxury B&Bs. They offer so much more than regular hotels. They are often decorated with exquisite antiques, and each room is different and special. Not only do you get a room to stay in; you get breakfast, which is usually a delicious home-cooked meal (often gourmet); and you get to talk to other people staying there. (How many times have you talked to people while staying at the Ritz Carlton? Not much, unless you hang out at the bar. Although sometimes that can be fun. Sipping a smooth martini or zesty margarita along with some snappy bar chat: "Hi, I'm Marilyn. If I was a guy, I'd want *me!*")

The other thing I love about B&Bs is that many of them have happy hours with free drinks and appetizers in the early evening. Sometimes, it's even enough for dinner! Besides which, they usually offer coffee, tea, soft drinks, and sometimes wine, as well as snacks at any time of day or night.

If you get a craving in the wee hours of the morn, you can just go to the lobby, snag a drink and cookies for free. That's a far cry from the minibar in a fancy hotel room, where you'll be charged $8 for a small bag of pretzels and $10 for a Diet Coke. At B&Bs, most of the time, it's all complimentary, not to mention most of them have free Internet, whereas at a hotel, you are often charged upwards of $9.95 a day! Sometimes the B&Bs have DVDs you can borrow or a piano you can play, or free magazines and books to read. Maybe they'll even have this one. If not, tell them to get it!

B&Bs run the gamut of prices from inexpensive to moderate to expensive to oh-my-gosh-you'd-have-to-be-a-millionaire! Whatever the cost, you generally get much more personal attention than at a hotel, and definitely more amenities. And most always, a lovely, delicious breakfast, if not that most appreciated and joyful happy hour.

Another benefit is that they are often located in non-touristy neighborhoods, where you'll find more authentic local eateries and shops. You can get the true flavor of the town you're visiting, instead of being in a sea of vacationers and getting overcharged at expensive tourist traps near the big hotels.

Add all the extra amenities up, and you are definitely getting a better deal at a B&B, and having a much better time. I've stayed at B&Bs all over the country: in New York City, San Francisco, Santa Barbara, La Jolla, Baton Rouge, New Orleans, Victoria, British Columbia, Carmel and Monterey, Philadelphia, and many other places, and I have loved them every time.

All B&B's Are Not the Same!

"Alright, Mom, I'll clean my room" –All kids everywhere

Okay, except one time. We were in Canada at an absolutely beautiful place. The rooms and grounds were so extraordinary they often had weddings there. The proprietress greeted us upon our arrival and seemed welcoming and pleasant. But when we got to our room, also gorgeous, with magnificent furnishings, there were little signs all over: "Take off your makeup before putting your head on the pillow." "Do not bring food into the room." "No breakfast after 9 a.m." "No TV after 9 p.m." "Do not take a bath after 10 p.m." "Do not talk too loud." "No bringing guests into your room."

Geez, I felt like I was a sorority girl and these were admonishments from the house mother! My boyfriend and I read all those notes and not only had to worry about talking too loud, we had to hold ourselves back from laughing too loud! That was the only time I didn't absolutely love the place or the people. But we had funny stories to tell afterwards, so it was worth it!

SITE: **www.bedandbreakfast.com**

Groupons, Living Social, and Yipit Travel Deals

These days, there are all kinds of deals in all kinds of places. **www.Groupon.com**, **www.LivingSocial.com**, and **www.Yipit.com** offer many travel getaways to all over the world. A myriad of different vacations are advertised on the sites. Watch for their discount days, too – when prices are even lower, such as when the sites offer an extra 20 to 30 percent off on their deals. Make sure you do your research on the place you're traveling to, whether it's a hotel or a city or country as well as the company that is featuring the offer. But, no question, there are a lot of excellent deals, be they hotel stays, B&B accommodations, or fully inclusive vacations with airfare and meals. Just be sure you know what the deal includes when you buy it. Read the offers carefully, including any fine print regarding dates, blackout times, and cancellation policies.

www.Travelzoo.com is another website that offers big deals on trips. Each week, they feature a Top 20 advertising the very best deals their staff has been able to discover from over 2,000 travel, entertainment and local businesses, including restaurants and spas. They have "Deal

Experts" worldwide who research, evaluate, negotiate, and test offers to find and confirm the best deals.

Cruisin' and Schmoozin'

Cruises offer a traveler a way to have everything included in one price, such as meals, entertainment and visiting different cities or countries all inclusive. Many people feel this gives them a true bang for their buck.

"What time is the midnight buffet?" –Anonymous

If you like to eat, you'll be in heaven, as cruises usually have delicious food, more food, and even more food. There are many eateries on cruise ships, most of which are included in the price – from casual to elegant, from sit-down to buffets. My main concern would be that I'd overeat and gain 20 pounds! But they also have gyms on board, or you can walk the decks or dance the night away to burn off those extra calories.

Keep in mind that there are cruise lines for different kind of travelers; some are more high-class and more expensive than others. Many cruise lines offer special discounts, and sometimes they can be booked through travel sites, clubs, or groups that give you additional discounts. I've never been on a cruise, since I don't like to be any place that, if I don't like it, I can't leave. Still, many people swear by this kind of vacation.

But what if you still can't afford it? Believe it or not, you can get a cruise for free, too! How? If you're an entertainer, like a singer or comic, many cruise lines will hire you – and pay you well to perform on their ships. I have a comedian friend who has been all over the world, making a fantastic living doing comedy on cruises. His career wasn't taking off in Los Angeles; he couldn't get bookings. But on cruises, he is one of the kings of comedy – always traveling, and being paid to do it. But, please be aware, you don't have to be a comic or a singer, either. Ships may want belly dancers, balloon twisters, arts and crafts instructors, poker instructors, face-painters, caricature artists, magicians, or any specialty others might find interesting that you can do or teach.

Speak to Me, Baby!

Cruises often book *enrichment speakers* or *destination speakers*. Sometimes, retirees or people retired from teaching or another career do these. It doesn't pay, but you will get an almost-free trip for you and possibly your spouse, speaking on a subject that's dear to your heart. This includes meals, travel, and an audience for your talks (if they don't walk out).

Sometimes, placement agencies hire the speakers; at other times, the cruise line itself does the hiring. Be sure you are a good speaker; you need entertainment value. Enrichment speakers talk about all kinds of topics: music, film, literature, photography, film, show business, or scientific subjects like oceanography, archaeology, you name it.

Destination speakers discuss different aspects of a given location, which might include its history, politics, arts and culture, wildlife and geography, as well as its cuisine. Of course, if you want to be on cruise ships all the time, they hire crew members for all kinds of jobs. But if you just want to go numerous times a year, you can try to become a speaker. It's not a paid position, but you get to travel and meet all kinds of people at no cost or low cost. So trade your love of a subject and ability to talk about it for some vacation time, cruising, and schmoozing. Check it out at:

http://www.wsj.com/articles/SB984592100527276224

http://www.cruisecritic.com/articles.cfm?ID=1176

Some places that hire speakers:

- Compass Speakers and Entertainment, Inc. – www.compassspeakers.com
- Posh Talks – poshtalks@aol.com
- Sixth Star Entertainment & Marketing – www.sixthstar.com
- To Sea With Z – www.toseawithz.com

Dancing on the Seas

Another way to get onto a cruise for free or at a low cost is if you're a good ballroom dancer. There are a lot of single people on cruises, especially women, so men are often welcomed if they can be a dancing escort. If you can teach ballroom dancing, or are a couple who ballroom dances, there are opportunities as well. These kinds of opportunities also pay a salary, but it means you'll probably be contracted for six months at a time to be on the ship.

"Make voyages! Attempt them . . . there's nothing else." –*Tennessee Williams*

Repositioning Cruises

A repositioning cruise (repo cruise) is a cruise in which the embarkation port and the disembarkation port are different. (They are usually on the "way back" from a cruise that takes people to popular destinations at seasonal times.) Frugal travelers often like these one-way cruises because they offer very reduced fares, compared to regular cruises. Most repositioning cruises are also longer, generally lasting more than a week, and they typically include more days at sea, rather than stops in various ports of call. Some people enjoy this, because it gives them more time to relax and take advantage of the things to do on board the ship. However, there are some negatives, such as having to fly one-way to the destination, and increased expenditures on the ship, because you are often on it longer.

http://www.repositioningcruise.com

http://cruises.lovetoknow.com/wiki/Repositioning_Cruises

Weekend at a Spa or Resort for Free

As with cruises, if you have an interesting subject you can talk about with authority, many fancy spas might host you for a few days in exchange for giving a talk. Likewise, if you have a skill or can teach guests a craft or activity. I knew a graphologist who would go to a spa every month for a weekend and teach people about graphology – or "read" their handwriting. She would get massages and facials at a wonderful spa every month. She was the most "relaxed" woman I've ever met! If you excel at a craft and can teach it, that might also work. Do you make jewelry, knit or crochet; or are you a master scrapbooker? See if a spa you want to visit would like you to teach a class one morning or afternoon in exchange for a short stay. I have also managed to get free trips to a fabulous spa by attending charity events. See the chapter on "Giving, Getting, and Gala-vanting."

If You Don't Play, You Can't Win

Enter those contests. Someone has to win, so why not YOU? There are all kinds of contests that award trips. You can find them all over. Whether you're out in the world or just at home on your computer, many travel websites and online magazines have sweepstakes. It doesn't cost anything to take a chance and fill out the form. My girlfriend went to the Los Angeles Travel Show, put her name in a bucket, and won a free trip to Italy.

Lots of radio stations offer trips as prizes when you donate during their membership drives. Not to mention, you can get dinners at restaurants, tickets to shows and, if you are truly lucky, maybe win the grand prize of a trip to Europe, Asia, or another exotic place.

In addition, some radio stations have contests just on regular days when you listen. Never doubt that someone will win – why not you? *Live! with Kelly* has a contest every morning wherein a viewer gets the chance to win a vacation if he or she correctly answers a question about the previous day's show. On week nights, *Wheel of Fortune* has an at-home winner who gets $5,000. Wowee – you could take an awesome trip if you won on that show.

I've actually won things myself; never a trip, but I once won a bicycle, and I also won an Asus Vivo Touchscreen Tablet by entering a contest at Bloomingdale's while I was shopping. Of course, I'd rather win a trip somewhere, but that hasn't happened *yet*. But you never know. You can't win if you don't play! So when you see those contests, give them your John Hancock! It's free to enter most of them . . . and you could end up going to some exotic land, totally free.

Be a Groupie

Another way to get inexpensive or even free trips is to gather a bunch of friends and book a tour. If you get a group together, sometimes YOUR trip is free. I have a friend who gets 15 singles together, and he gets his trip FREE. Even if it's not free, create a group, and you'll travel for less. Or you can join an existing group. Be resourceful. Do you belong to a women's group? A men's club? A baby boomers' group, or a "loves to travel" club? If they don't have one near you, start one. There are also lots of Meetup groups all over the country. Find one near you at **www.meetup.com**. There are also lots of travel clubs or groups everywhere. Not only will your trip cost less, you'll meet other folks who like to travel like you do.

Travel Agents

There's no question that the burgeoning Internet has taken over a niche that used to be handled by travel agents. In the past, if you wanted to book a trip, you definitely called a travel agent. Now, there are so many more options at your fingertips with all kinds of travel sites and individual hotels, airlines and destinations providing booking right over the web. However, travel agents are still operating, and many offer things that going directly to the web doesn't. Because it's their everyday business, they are often privy to places and prices that ordinary people don't know about.

At a recent event I attended, a travel agent showed the audience how going through *her* to book a trip could save many thousands of dollars, as well as get some inside information on the specific destinations. It doesn't cost you anything to check out what a travel agent has to offer. Again, it's about doing your research and then deciding what route is best for you, i.e., the route of *Do It Yourself*, or letting a travel professional book your trip.

Timeshare Rentals

Another relatively inexpensive way to get a nice vacation stay is checking for timeshares for rent. There are numerous sites that offer rentals at a discount from the company or the owner of the timeshare.

http://www.redweek.com/timeshare-rentals

http://www.timeshare-resale-rental.com/timeshare-rentals

In addition to the possibility of renting a timeshare, many timeshare companies offer you a free weekend if you go to hear their sales pitch. Plus, they offer other prizes, too. This is common for a number of resorts in Las Vegas, Orlando, Hawaii, and other popular vacation areas. There are lots of folks who go to the presentations just to get the freebies offered. If you don't mind spending (or wasting) two to three hours listening to the pitch, there are some wonderful places to go and free gifts to be had. Be careful, though, that you don't get talked into buying something you don't want. Their pitchmen are masters of high pressure tactics that will entice you to snatch up their deal-of-the-century. So, before you go, practice saying "No!" Renting a timeshare that someone else owns is most often a better choice.

Fly Me to the Moon – or Somewhere Not Quite as Far

"My fear of flying starts as soon as I buckle myself in and then the guy up front mumbles a few unintelligible words. Then, before I know it, I'm thrust into the back of my seat by acceleration that seems way too fast and the rest of the trip is an endless nightmare of turbulence, of near misses. And then the cabbie drops me off at the airport." –Dennis Miller

Air Travel

Points, Points, and More Points . . .

Most airlines have frequent flyer programs, but traveling is only one way to get points toward free trips. **Credit cards** and other promotional cards give you points to use for travel, hotels, and other items, too. There are many credit cards that offer you anywhere from 10,000 to 50,000 miles for free if you register for their card and spend a certain amount in the first few months. Often, these cards waive the annual fee the first year. I sign up for the card and then cancel after the first year. I've amassed over 100,000 miles opening new credit cards, then canceling before it was renewed with a fee. Apologies to Suze Orman, who would probably say not to do this, because it could lower your credit rating. Still, it's something with which I've had success, and my rating is excellent. Keep your eyes open to see what various cards offer, and then combine them with your favorite airline to get trips for free!

Keep in mind some frequent flyer programs have a time limit on when the points or miles expire, so pay attention and don't lose your hard-earned miles. If you can't use them, they may be transferrable, and you might be able to gift them or sell them. Check out these sites or their newsletters for lots of tips, offers, and information on where to get deals:

www.frequentflier.com

www.flyertalk.com

There are also sites that compare air fares and those that predict airfares so you'll know the best time to book your travel. These sites do that, as well as offer other info and ways to book the cheapest flights.

www.momondo.com

www.skyscanner.com

www.airwatchdog.com

www.farecompare.com

www.kayak.com

And if you're a student, check out: **www.studentuniverse.com**

"What does it mean to pre-board? Do you get on before you get on?" –George Carlin

Complain, It Helps! (Or If You're Jewish – Stretch Your Kvetch!)

I was taking what I thought would be a regular, uneventful but long cross-country flight. Before the plane took off, the flight attendant came over with a little five-year-old girl. The attendant said she was asked to take care of the young child, but had flight duties, so could she put her next to me and could I watch her? How could I say no? I smiled and helped to buckle her in. The flight took off and the little girl started kicking the seat in front of her. The man in the seat turned around to me and glared. "Will you please keep your daughter still!" I gave a little shrug. "Uh . . . sure, except she's not my daughter." The girl kept squirming the whole time, and I tried to quiet her by doing finger puppets, funny noises, talking like a duck, you name it. Before landing, the stewardess (I know it's not PC, but this woman doesn't deserve PC) moved the little girl to sit next to her in a row closer to the front.

As I was deplaning I saw the flight attendant bring the girl to her parents. The parents gave the attendant a huge bouquet of roses and showered her with praise and gratitude. I was thinking, "Hey, I was the one that took care of your little demon. You should be giving *me* the flowers and praise." But I didn't say that. And as I passed the flight attendant, she gave me a wide smile and held up her bouquet. It gnawed at me that night, so I decided to write to the airline. I explained what had happened and told them I should've been paid for baby-sitting services! They responded with a free round trip ticket anywhere they fly! My letter worked and showed it's sometimes smart to complain.

Bitchin' and Moanin' Fer All to Hear

These days, it often *pays to complain in public*. People who post their complaints online, whether on Yelp, Twitter, or YouTube sometimes get results really fast. One guy wrote a song complaining about an airline; he played his guitar and sang on YouTube, and it went viral. He not only got results, he got his "10 minutes of fame" getting on various TV talk shows, too. And of course, they flew him there free to be on the shows.

"You want to know what it's like to be on a plane for 22 hours? Sit in a chair, squeeze your head as hard as you can, don't stop, then take a paper bag and put it over your mouth and nose and breathe your own air over and over and over." –Lewis Black

Flattery Will Get You Everywhere . . . or Maybe Something Extra

In other cases, praise may work better than complaints. My friend John went to the Outback, and got money back. He was on his way to Australia, but got to the plane late.

At the security checkpoint, they called the pilot to hold the plane and told John to run! He did, and managed to make the plane, but his luggage wasn't going to make it with him. The airline attendants told him to go to the lost luggage department when he arrived in Australia, and that the representatives there would get his bags to him at his hotel. His flight was 15 hours long, and the crew who waited for him gave him special treatment.

When he landed, he went to the lost luggage area as instructed and filled out the forms, all the while complimenting the agent about the airline. Initially, she offered John $100 for clothing and amenities until his luggage could get to him. He kept praising the airline in his charming way, and she upped the offer, saying she would give him $150. John was in such a great frame of mind from the trip that he continued complimenting the airline, till finally she said, "Okay I'll give you $200, but that's the limit that I can give you."

He gratefully accepted and began his Australian trip with an extra $200! So in this case, instead of complaining, praising them got him a nice bonus.

Helpful Hints for Saving When Traveling:

- Book really early or book really late

- Use a credit card that pays back cash or miles

- Redeem frequent flyer points for miles and hotels

- Book tours in each country *when you get there*, rather than in advance. It's often much cheaper than if you book from the U.S.

- Volunteer to get bumped from your flight. If you book your trip at a busy time, chances are it might be an overbooked flight. You'll go on the next flight out and get a free ticket to use another time.

- Avoid single supplements, check travel mates sites. Go for less, and make a new friend.

- Travel ON a holiday. Flights are usually crowded and expensive around holidays like Thanksgiving, Xmas, and New Year's. But if you travel on the actual day, it's usually cheaper. Plus, you often get really good service and hospitality.

- Fly from or to a nearby airport, maybe 30 or 40 miles away. Flights are often cheaper at more out-of-the way airports. For example, instead of LAX, fly from John Wayne Airport in Orange County, or even from Burbank.

- Sign up for emails and newsletters from the airlines you like to travel. You'll get special offers and deals.

- Spirit Airlines supposedly offers $9 flights if you become a member. Frontier Airlines offers lots of inexpensive fares, especially if you become a member of their Discount Den, such as a $15 flight from Los Angeles to Las Vegas. JetBlue is also known to have good prices. Southwest's Click 'n Save is another place for promotions.

- Carry your baggage and check it at the gate. Now, with airlines charging for bags, even cheap fares can add up and up and up. If you carry your bag and it's too big, often at the gate, they will check it . . . and there, it won't cost you anything.

- Join loyalty programs from hotel chains. You'll get extra days, upgrades, and discounts.

- Travel off-season.

- Travel on the best days of the week: https://www.kayak.com/news/best-time-book-travel/

- Nonrefundable fares are not really nonrefundable. (Stan, a friend of mine, says he books a fare, then cancels it within 24 hours, and makes another reservation the next day. He keeps doing this until he gets the best fare. I wouldn't have the patience or fortitude to do this, but he swears he's gotten some amazing airfares this way.)

More Websites for Travel Tips

www.frommers.com

www.lonelyplanet.com

www.smartertravel.com/travel-advice

www.ricksteves.com/travel-tips

www.traveladvice.com

www.travelsense.org/tips/index.cfm

www.Tripadvisor.com

Consider Instagram for tips, too. I know it's filled with other people's travel pix, but they also offer inside info, like a favorite restaurant, hotel, day excursions, etc. Explore it for all the golden nuggets of helpful information.

Facebook. Yes, it's usually used for people sharing photos of their lunch and pets, but there are groups of all kinds on there, too. These days it's easier than ever to make friends all over the globe. It's at your fingertips. Join groups centered on travel or living in the places that you want to visit. You may make connections even before you go. You'll have hosts or friends to show you around when you get there. Linkedin is for business, but who's to say you can't meet business contacts when you travel, too?

Don't Take Candy from a Stranger – But How about a FREE TRIP?

You never know how an opportunity may present itself. Here are some wild examples of how people got free trips:

"Are you named Elizabeth Gallagher (and Canadian?) Want a free plane ticket around the world?"

That was the posting on Reddit made by Jordan Axani from Toronto, who purchased a "wicked trip around the world" for him and his girlfriend. The trip was nonrefundable, so when they broke up, he did the best thing he could. He offered the trip free to anyone who had a Canadian passport and the *same name* as his ex! He got dozens of responses and chose one to go on a trip of a lifetime.

A jilted groom in England, John Whitbread, auctioned off his ex-fiancée's ticket on eBay and donated some of the proceeds to charity. He got worldwide coverage of his story and became a bit of a celebrity.

What is it with these guys? Why don't they pick the right women?

Another hubby-to-be ditched at the altar was Franz Wizner. Instead of brooding about his runaway bride and a demotion at work, he decided to spend his two-week honeymoon in Costa Rica with his brother. The two of them ended up quitting their jobs and traveling for two years through 53 countries. He wrote a book about it, *Honeymoon with My Brother*, which became a *New York Times* bestseller and landed him guest spots on *Oprah* and *The Today Show*. In addition, Sony Pictures purchased the movie rights.

Bottom line – all of these people had something they wanted to do. They didn't know when they started how it was going to turn out. But they took a chance. They were open to the possibilities, stayed flexible, and ended up having the experience of a lifetime. Sometimes they even got rich or famous along the way. It just goes to show . . . *you never know!*

> **"I haven't been everywhere, but it's on my list." –Susan Sontag**

Car Talk

> **"Women are like cars: we all want a Ferrari, sometimes want a pickup truck, and end up with a station wagon." –Tim Allen**

Do you get jealous when you see someone in the lane next to you in a Ferrari, Rolls Royce or Lamborghini? How would YOU like to be that guy or gal? You don't have to be a millionaire . . . if it's just for a week or weekend. There are many luxury car rental services all over the country. So you don't have to *buy* the car – just drive it when the mood strikes.

www.laluxurycarrental.com

www.gothamdreamcars.com

https://exoticcars.enterprise.com

http://www.apexluxurycarhire.com

"Kilometers are shorter than miles. Save gas, take your next trip in kilometers." –George Carlin.

Start Your Engines

There are also Exotic Car Sharing Clubs. When you become a member, you get the use of a variety of exotic, sports, vintage and specialty cars when you want them. An added benefit is getting to meet other auto enthusiasts in the club. Again, you don't have to *buy* these expensive beauties to be able to experience them.

http://www.exoticcarshare.com/

There are numerous other Car Clubs like **https://www.clubsportiva.com/** that not only offer rentals, but Exotic Car Tours where you get to drive six different exotic and luxury cars over 120 miles or seven towns along with other participants. Needless to say, this would make a phenomenal gift for any car enthusiast.

"I had to stop driving my car for a while . . . the tires got dizzy." –Steven Wright

Speaking of car sharing, it's something you can do even for a regular get-around-town type of car. What if you don't own a car, or just need one for a couple of hours? Instead of taking a taxi or bus, or even Uber or Lyft – you can use **www.zipcar.com**. This company offers automobile reservations to its members, billable by the day or hour. Another site is **www.turo.com**. This is a site for renting a car from private parties, and you'll have your choice of a luxury car or a beater! You can even list your own car that you don't use a lot – and *make some money* for yourself.

Auto-Lover Snippet

I was at an elegant party at a Jaguar dealer and gave them my business card indicating I was a travel reporter. The marketing gal invited me to drive an Austin Healy convertible free for two weeks if I'd write an article about it. I'm not much for sports car driving, so I never contacted her. About a hundred guys I've met think I'm the dumbest person in the world! But if you're a car fanatic, start writing about them. One friend of mine wrote for numerous car magazines. He was literally given a different free car to drive every week!

"I'm so naive about finances. Once when my mother mentioned an amount, and I realized I didn't understand, she had to explain: 'That's like three Mercedes.' Then I understood." –Brooke Shields

Leave the Driving to Us . . . While YOU Relax on the Bus

Do you have a fear of flying? But you hate the stress of driving? Since I've covered planes and cars, what about the bus? Lux Bus is an upscale bus service that operates between Los Angeles, Anaheim and Las Vegas. However, it's not cheap. One way to Vegas starts at $65, Round trip at $98. I'd rather use that money for something fun when I get there. What's a girl to do? How about spending one dollar instead?

I'm not kidding . . . *you can book a bus for only $1!* Check out **www.Boltbus.com**. They operate on the West Coast in Los Angeles, Las Vegas, San Francisco, Seattle, Portland, and Vancouver and on the East Coast in NYC, NJ, Boston, Philadelphia and Washington DC. Depending on when and where you book it, someone always gets a seat for $1. Sometimes it's $2 or a little more. I booked a ticket from LA to Las Vegas for $3. I was meeting my boyfriend, who was driving from San Francisco. We were meeting in Vegas, and he was driving back to LA with me. Taking the Boltbus was a helluva lot cheaper than $89 for a flight or $65 on the Lux Bus. It also beats Amtrak prices if you're traveling between D.C. and New York.

> **"Lots of people want to ride with you in the limo, but what you want is someone who will take the bus with you when the limo breaks down." –Oprah Winfrey**

In or Out of Town, Apps Can Help

Whether you're in your hometown, or playing tourist somewhere, there are lots of helpful travel apps. Want to avoid current traffic problems? Try **www.waze.com**. This is an app that gathers real-time movement data to calculate traffic delays on your route.

Another app that's useful whether you're a resident or visitor is **www.localeur.com.** It focuses on local experiences, recommended by people living in that city. Each writer has a profile and a photo explaining who they are and what kind of interests they have. It might be favorite dance hangouts, or places for terrific food or drinks, or preferred spots for art, music, etc.

A Final Travel Tip

Don't forget, once you get to where you're going and have a hotel, check the other chapters to find out how to get the shows, attractions, restaurants and shopping that a millionaire would *love* but *YOU* can afford.

> **"The world is a book, and those who do not travel read only a page."** –Saint Augustine

Chap Wrap 'n Recap

- Travel Reporting
- Blog It or Vlog It
- Free Spain for a Week
- Volunteer Ops for Travel
- Home Swapping and Couch Flopping
- Air BnB and Other B&Bs
- Groupons, Living Social and Yipit
- Cruising-on-the-Cheap
- Air Travel Tips and Sites
- Luxury Buses and Exotic Cars

Trippin' 'n Quippin' Quiz – True or False

1. On Cheepy-Deepy Air, you don't pay extra for bags – you just put them on the roof rack.
2. Writing a travel column or blog can get you a trip, a dinner, or a high colonic.
3. The most economical way to fly from Los Angeles to Las Vegas is by hover board.
4. You can get a six-night stay at a four-star-resort in Spain just by talking and being your charming self.
5. To spend a week driving a Ferrari or Lamborghini, you need to spend a year's salary.
6. If you teach origami, haiku, or feng shui, you might get a weekend at a spa or a punch in the nose.

7. Feathering your Nest with the Best

"Decorate your home – it gives the illusion that your life is more interesting than it really is." –Charles M. Schultz

Home is Where the ART Is

Your home reflects who you are. If you put things that you love in it, and create an environment in which you are comfortable and happy, you will feel rich, even if you're not.

Decorating is personal, and so is your taste. You can benefit from other people who have the same taste and paid retail, but pay a whole lot less. Here are some ideas for you to jazz up your space at a fraction of retail prices.

How to Get a $10,000 Sofa . . . for $200

I recently found out I have to move from where I've lived for 20 years. Eeeek. What am I going to do? What if my furniture doesn't fit in the new place? What if it doesn't look good there? I want NEW furniture to go with my NEW place.

Maybe you're not moving, but you just want to redecorate or create some new feng shui. But where can you get quality furniture that doesn't cost a fortune? Craigslist? Maybe. On the sidewalk? Maybe not! But you'll never know unless you look. One of the best kept secrets is thrift stores run by charities. The secret is to find thrift shops in a neighborhood where rich people donate.

Think about it. Millionaires don't have time to sell their things, and they don't want strangers walking through their houses. So they take their furniture to a consignment store, or just donate it and get a tax deduction. Which means *you* can luck out and find incredible furnishings and other great things for super low prices! Many of the thrift stores operate for charities, so you'll be helping others as you buy. Disabled Veterans' Charities, St. Vincent de Paul, and Salvation Army are a few of the shops available. My favorite is the Jewish Women's Council Thrift Shop.

Here are some examples:

I was looking for a white couch. I looked all over: at department stores, furniture stores, online, at warehouses, you name it. Unfortunately, the only couches I liked were waaaaaay over what I could afford.

Then I popped into my favorite thrift shop one day. VOILA! I walked in and saw this gorgeous, pristine white sofa. It probably cost about $10,000 new. It was so perfect it must have been sitting in a living room that no one ever went into!

I had to ask how much, and I was prepared to negotiate. But when the sales clerk said $200, I didn't *need* to negotiate. Wow, what a find! I quickly paid for it and made arrangements for delivery. The next day I invited a girlfriend over to my apartment and showed it to her. She couldn't believe I'd found this stunning couch at a thrift shop. What's more, she insisted I get the matching chair. I rushed back to the store, and *my* chair was still there. It was a not-so-whopping $60. At the same time, they had a magnificent formal dining table with six chairs for a ridiculously low price, but it was too big to fit into my apartment. These items obviously came from the home of someone quite wealthy who either moved (good luck in your new home!) or redecorated (I can't wait to catch you next time around!) or died (So sorry, condolences, but thanks for thinking of me!)

Of course, after I bought the white couch, I realized the problem with it. It looked so clean and white I didn't want anyone to sit on it! I called it the Forbidden Zone. When people come over, they can look, but they can't sit! (If you're old enough, maybe you remember how in the 1950s, people used to put plastic slipcovers over furniture. It always stayed nice and clean, but it was sticky and icky to sit on.)

By the way, I wasn't far off in how much I thought it originally cost. How did I find out? When I was searching through the pillows for loose change my boyfriend had dropped, I found an old receipt taped on the frame under the seat cushions. $9,759.99. Wow, was I close!

Be Nifty, Shop Thrifty!

Here are some of the other marvelous pieces I've bought at my favorite thrift shop. I found a super-looking leather recliner that would normally cost $650, and I got it for $75. I found paintings, a set of solid oak shelves, an ultra-cool wine rack and a beautiful chandelier that were all less than $10 each! I go into that thrift shop every month or so just to look. They always have the most extraordinary furnishings, so I keep wanting to redo my apartment over and over! Of course, I don't do it, but I will often call friends to tell them about pieces I see that they might want.

It's important to remember that thrift stores can be hit or miss, and that some are better than others. Find the ones in the neighborhoods that you like. Some others that you might try: Out of the Closet, American Cancer Discovery Shop, and Goodwill. Goodwill even has an online presence at **www.ShopGoodwill.com**. It's like eBay, but it's the first Internet action site created, owned, and operated by a nonprofit.

Again, don't forget that with thrift shops, you have to keep stopping by. It's a matter of timing. You need to check back often till you find the things that call out to you. I once found an artsy table that three people offered to buy from me when I was in the cashier line. As I went to pay for it, the others tried to start a bidding war. However, the clerk said I got to it first. Timing is everything!

Who knows – you might even find some little *objet d'art* that ends up being worth a million dollars.

Yard, Garage, and Estate Sales

If you watch *Antiques Roadshow*, you are probably a treasure hunter and know you can find many wonderful things at sales in your local area. Even better, when you travel, these kinds of yard and garage sales can be amazing, especially in out of the way places not frequented by the usual pack of savvy buyers.

There is definitely strategy involved with yard, garage and estate sales. Go early to get first dibs on the selection, and come at the end to get leftovers for an even better deal. Of course, at the end you only get what's left over. The good news is that, by then, they sometimes even give it away for free!

Lake Arrowhead is a scenic mountain resort in the San Bernardino Mountains, east of Los Angeles. Every Memorial Day and Labor Day weekend, they have massive garage sales for all the "flatlanders" who come up for the weekend. There are dozens if not hundreds of these sales, all with their own treasures. (Sometimes they even have cars, boats, and houses for sale.) More often, when I visit friends in San Diego on a weekend, there are always yard sales dotting the streets, and my car automatically stops at every one!

Sometimes, sellers have a sentimental connection to the wares offered, so watch how you barter. Remember that negotiation is an art. It takes practice, but it can be fun. Try it; you have nothing to lose, and you might get a real bargain! Ask them for a price first, so you have an idea of what they want. Sometimes, it's much cheaper than you would have offered. Then haggle away!

Remember ABC – Always Bring Cash! Also, you should have a checkbook or credit card back up, although some sellers won't accept anything but good old-fashioned bucks.

Hop to a Prop Shop

Here in Los Angeles, we are blessed with some great prop houses that get items from the studios. Some sell retail to the public, too, so you have to check and see. But you might be able to purchase some cool items that have been featured in one of your favorite shows or movies!

Check online in your city for prop houses or rental places that might have great trinkets and treasures. There are small theaters in every city, so they have to get their furniture and props from somewhere. Just call and ask if they sell items in addition to renting them.

There's a Flea in My Swap

Every city or town often has a specific area for swap meets or flea markets. In Los Angeles they do it up big at the Rose Bowl. There are also community colleges and schools that hold them on weekends in their parking lots, and some cities even have permanent locations. It's amazing that you find just what you were looking for and a whole lot of other stuff that you weren't, but suddenly can't live without! Bring cash and a checkbook as backup, in case you find something big that you didn't expect but really, really want.

Outlets and Sidewalk Sales

Lots of regular furniture stores have outlets where they sell items that have been returned, floor samples, or slightly soiled items, etc. Big retailers like Sears and Macy's have them, as do Z Gallerie, Pampa, Furniture2Go, and many others. Sometimes, expensive shops even have sidewalk sales where you can find amazing bargains.

Neat and Sweet Hotel Suite Treats

Most people don't think that hotels ever change their furnishings, but they do, regularly. So they sell everything in really good shape, usually every two to four years. You can find some five-star chains that unload thousands of pieces of furniture and decorative items really cheap! Contact your favorite chains and find out their schedule. Ask where they sell the fabulous offerings from their properties. Then get some great finds at great discount prices. On furniture, artwork, glassware and china, linens, electronics, and more! You can also Google "hotel furniture" or "hotel outlets" in your area.

http://www.hotelsurplus.com/

http://www.hotelfurnitureguy.com/

https://besthotelproducts.com/

www.wayfairsupply.com/hotel

Rental Outlets

As with hotel outlets, businesses that rent furniture, such as Cort and Brook Furniture Rental, also sell their furniture. You can call to find out when and where.

https://www.cort.com/furniture-clearance

http://www.bfr.com/furniture-rental/clearance-center/

http://www.afrcc.com/

https://www.aarons.com/t-howtoownit.aspx

Consignment and Used Furniture Stores

Much like the charity stores, it's about visiting often and building a relationship with the sales people. Let them know what you are looking for and stop by often. Wertz Brothers Furniture in West Los Angeles has a 55,000 square foot showroom where it's fun to browse, even if you're not in the market to buy.

Buy. Sell. Repeat.

Another thing to keep in mind about buying used furniture is that at a later date, you can sell it! When I first moved to Los Angeles, I needed some furniture fast. I perused the ads in the local newspaper (this was pre-Craigslist) and bought a used couch for $50, a glass coffee table for $60, and a cushioned armchair for $25. When I moved from that apartment five years later, I sold the couch for $160, the table for $100 and the chair for $50. Not bad, huh? The point is, if you get a terrific bargain, you may even be able to sell it at a profit. (What do you think used furniture stores do?) My friend Michael bought a desk for $70 and sold it a few months later for $400! This is also what sellers on eBay do. Buy low and sell high. (Good advice for the stock market, too!)

Online Deals

www.Amazon.com, www.eBay.com, and www.Overstock.com are just a few of the many websites where you can find deals on furniture and home décor. www.Wayfair.com offers lots of furnishings with high discounts; although I've never used them, I'm on their mailing list, and have seen some terrific offers.

Craigslist is another great option. They have furniture listings, and even a section where people are *giving things away free!* Sometimes these giveaways can be good; people who are moving from apartments have to get rid of everything in them, and if they can't sell their heavy items, they often just want someone to come and take them away. Sometimes they'll tell you the items are out front on the curb!

Whether you're getting a good price or a "steal" on something, make sure to bring a friend with you. If you're buying, a friend can provide another opinion, but no matter what, you should always use caution in going to a stranger's home, or in letting anyone you don't know into yours. If it sounds waaaay too good to be true, it probably is. In looking for apartments on Craigslist or other real estate sites, I can always judge when something is fake or a fraud. If apartments are half the price of other similar ones in the same neighborhood, I don't trust that it's for real. On the other hand, sometimes you just luck out and get something amazing for an amazingly low price. Just remember, whatever you do, be smart and be safe.

Other sites where you can buy and sell used furniture online:

> www.Chairish.com
>
> www.Letgo.com
>
> www.Offerup.com
>
> www.Viyet.com

There are also pawn shops all over, though I've never bought anything from them.

Green Thumbs and Brown Fingers

Plants are another way to decorate a home and make it look fabulous. They don't have to be expensive, but they can last a long time and create a wonderful atmosphere. Just make sure you have a green thumb. Mine isn't green; I'd kill a *fake* plant if it were possible. Nonetheless, because I'm terrible at keeping plants up, I buy artificial trees at Michael's – they look wonderful, and don't require watering. Just a quick friendly dust, and they're fine – and I don't have to worry about overwatering and having leaky, muddy water to sop up from the rug underneath the pot.

Summer, Winter, Spring or Fall

One final thought about buying furniture is to think seasonally. After the holidays, winter savings are offered. After the Fourth of July, summer things go on sale. After Labor Day, summer leftovers can be half price or less. If you are lucky to live where the actual summer weather lasts till December, take advantage of the deals, and still use them this year. If you don't mind storing your deals till the season rolls around again, stock up, and you'll be ready for next year in style for less!

In any case, be a savvy buyer. Do your research before you go into the seller's territory, and you will know the value of the treasures you seek. Then you can bargain and get deals that you will love for years to come.

Fabulous Fabric

My old roommate in New York was a super creative gal who had taken interior design classes. Together, we came up with many imaginative ways to decorate our apartment. We had found an old chest of drawers that was tremendously functional, but horribly ugly. Carole had a great idea. She bought some really cool fabric in contrasting colors. Armed with just scissors and glue, we covered the top, sides and frame of the chest with the red patterned fabric and the drawers with the matching beige patterned fabric. It came out absolutely fabulous. Everyone wanted to know where we'd gotten such a beautiful chest of drawers that must've cost a bundle. When we told folks we'd made it, they were shocked. We probably could've taken orders to make and sell them, but we were both busy with furthering our careers in show biz. Along with the chest of drawers that Carole covered, we used other patterned fabric for different things. I placed fabric on canvas stretchers to make artwork. A large painting might be expensive, but get a couple yards of a cool fabric, and you can make a fantastic wall hanging!

I also use patterned sheets for originality, style, and economy. Fancy comforters or bedspreads can be expensive. Instead, I buy a couple sets of sheets with an awesome design. I'll put one of the sheets on top of the bedclothes instead of a bedspread. Then I cover the two night tables (old and basic) with the matching sheets. It looks amazing, and it's easy to change my colors often by using different sheets. You can also use sheets to make eye-catching drapes to match or not match. Friends always want to see my bedroom, because it's always beautiful, colorful and special. Or maybe the guys want to see it for another reason? In any case, I have fun doing some artsy things that always get compliments.

Also, if you're good at painting, you can paint cool designs on furniture and turn it into something new. Check craft stores for decals, decorations, and info on how to do things. Michael's is a wonderful crafts store where you can get ideas. Don't forget to look at home decorating magazines, too. You can see what rich people are buying, and copy it with less expensive things. Adding colorful pillows or decorative doodads can make a bland piece of furniture look totally different.

Treasures and Trinkets Galore

You might have your home full of furniture, but it's not really a home unless you make it yours. You can do this with art, wall hangings, knickknacks, and ornaments. I personally think this is what stands out in any person's home or office. We get a sense of who they are by seeing the things they have, the art on the wall, the books on the shelves, the items on counters, tables, etc. It's what makes your place your *palace*. Even if it's only a studio apartment!

Did you ever go to someone's home and notice that they have a collection of specific things in a corner or on a shelf? One girl I knew had thousands of Barbie dolls. Thousands, really! In every room of her house! They were probably worth a lot of money, but I thought it a little over the top for my taste. Some people have glass bottles, or Russian nesting dolls, or eclectic things from their travels. It's always fun to see what is important to folks and what decorative touches they've used.

If you come to my place, you'll notice a few different things. After I wrote my first book, *Never Kiss a Frog: A Girl's Guide to Creatures from the Dating Swamp*, everyone started giving me frogs. Ceramic frogs, glass frogs, wooden frogs, stuffed frogs, big frogs, and little frogs. I had frogs on my desk, on my kitchen counter, on living room shelves and bedroom chairs. Everyone knew me as the "frog lady." It was fine with me, because it was a way to keep my book *hopping* and out in the public eye, and it was really part of who I was. Finally, I had to tell people to stop giving me frogs or I would croak! But for a while, it was fun to see the collection grow. Of course, I've kissed too many *human* frogs, which is what the book is about.

DAE DIY? – Does Anyone Else Do It Yourself?

The other thing you'll find in my apartment is all kinds of creative art that I've made. For one of my boyfriends, I took pages out of the Fredericks of Hollywood catalog. Then I put MY HEAD on all the bodies! I made a fantastic collage out of it and hung it in my bedroom. I'm not with him anymore (he's a frog), but let me tell you, whenever guests come to my apartment and see that collage, they remark on what a fantastic body I have! Yes, all the figures are in hot lingerie . . . with my head placed in the perfect positions right on top of them. I bet a Van Gogh painting over my bed wouldn't get half the attention my collage does!

I've made collages as presents, too. If you don't have a lot of money to spend on gift-giving, making something personal often says more than something you've bought from a store. For a friend's bridal shower, I made a special couple's collage. My girlfriend and her fiancé were both in show business, so I cut out photos of all the famous happy couples in television land, like Lucy & Desi, The Honeymooners, the Cleavers, and the Pritchetts and Dunphys from Modern Family. I put their photos around the sides, each with a caption below indicating how many years they'd been together. In the middle was a large photo of a bride and groom with my girlfriend and her boyfriend's heads on them, with the heading, "Forever." I framed it and presented it along with a poem I wrote to go with it. When the bride-to-be opened the collage at the party, everyone "oohed and ahhed," and it was a major hit. So much so that one of the other women asked if she could buy one from me as a gift for another girlfriend of hers!

I love making funny collages, whether for myself or as gifts. It's enjoyable to do, and they're always appreciated when people see them or receive them. I'm not a real artist, but it doesn't matter; it's the personal touch and thought that counts. All it takes is some photos, some scissors and some creativity. Try it!

If you're not artistic, but need some help – a good place to find artists is on **www.fiverr.com** or **www.upwork.com**. If you need someone to help to put furniture together or even to construct something new, you can try **www.craigslist.com**, **www.taskrabbit.com**, or **www.handy.com**.

Found Objects

> One person's junk is another person's treasure. –Old idiom

One of my favorite places to go is the Gallery of Functional Art in Santa Monica. Just like it sounds, this is a shop where all the items are not only useful, but are visually imaginative and classify as art. I'm always interested to see how "pros" create or decorate regular furniture or household items and make them special and beautiful. This gallery has all kinds of furnishings and lighting, as well as glassware, ceramics, and jewelry that are made in unique ways and run the gamut from folk to fantasy, comfortable to conceptual, and minimalist to complex. I've seen furniture there made from wine corks, cardboard boxes, newspapers, metal scraps, bottle caps, all kinds of things. If they can do it, you can, too, if you think outside the box. I'm still trying to figure out how to make something from all those cardboard bathroom toilet rolls that get thrown away. Now *that* would be some useful recycling!

On the Street Where You Live . . . or Don't

I remember when I was in college and a big thing with students was to make coffee tables from wooden spools we got at construction sites. Although I'm past that phase now, I always think about creative ways to make new things that look special and eclectic in my home. When I lived in West Los Angeles, outside my apartment was an old, horribly rusted fire extinguisher. It didn't work, and it looked so terrible it could almost be classified as an eyesore. I had heard that some people made fire extinguishers into lamps, i.e., using the metal extinguisher as the base of a lamp. I got a tarnish remover and started rubbing and rubbing, and rub-a-dub-dubbing. Because it was so corroded, it was taking forever. It probably was better than lifting barbells for my arm muscles. Finally, I gave up and took it to a place called Art in Metal, and they just "dipped" it. When I picked it up a week later, OMG, I had a stunning, shiny copper and brass ornament for my floor that gets compliments whenever people see it. It cost about $50 to do and was well worth it.

I've also repurposed things such as an old wire cassette holder, which I turned into a jewelry rack, by hanging earrings and necklaces on it. This one-of-a-kind jewelry stand looks great on my bureau and makes it easy to find the baubles I'm going to wear every day.

If You Can't Afford *Expensive* – Try *Unusual*

Both with furniture and accessories, if you can't afford high-priced things, try unique things. When something is different or offbeat, it stands out and can look expensive even if it isn't. No one will be able to tell how much it cost. **www.Etsy.com** is a great website for finding lots of artistic home-made items from different artists, designers and craftsmen.

Speaking of "found objects," New York City used to be a haven for finding the coolest of cool things on the sidewalks. I'm not sure if it still is, but I know many people who discovered sensational things for their home. My friend, Dan, told me he furnished his whole apartment from the street; he found couches, tables, humidifiers, and artwork, all of it fabulous. In fact, he even found a young woman on the sidewalk, and took her home and married her! I think it's the one thing he found there that he wanted to take back.

What About FREE?

Yep, there are even ways to get cool furniture for free.

Dumpster diving isn't for me, but there are people who do it and love it. There are TV shows about it and stories of men who make a veritable fortune selling things they've found. Still, I'd hardly call dumpster diving living like a millionaire. But hey, I won't knock it if you can dive for it and turn your trash into cash!

You can also sometimes get good pieces for free from craigslist.com. They have a free section, and sometimes when people are moving, they don't have an interest in selling, or time to take their items to a Goodwill store or other charity shop. So they will list it for FREE on Craigslist. All you have to do is pick it up.

In addition, some "green" non-profits offer you a way to pick up used furniture or items to prevent them from contributing to landfill waste. Donation Nation is a green removal and redistribution service that allows you to pick up one free piece of furniture or box of items once a week:

http://www.donationnationusa.org/Redistribution.html

JSYN . . . More DIY – Just So You Know . . . More Do It Yourself

Doing it yourself is not a bad thing. Just ask Martha Stewart. She is a billionaire from doing things herself, and showing others how. They even have entire cable TV channels based on this. If there's something you can do yourself, it's somewhere on the Internet. Often a quick search of Google or YouTube will get you many "how to" ideas. There are videos showing you how to tie a tie, frame a picture, paint a painting, design artwork, bake a pie, or change a tire. You can learn how to make a chair, construct a desk, design a sofa, or build a log cabin. (You can also watch pimple-popping videos, but I don't recommend those, unless you love getting grossed out!)

Don't be afraid to try to do something creative. With a little insight and perseverance, you can do amazing things to decorate your home.

Some popular DIY sites:

www.DIYnetwork.com

www.Doityourself.com

www.Easy2diy.com

Design and Art School Students

There are schools all over the country that teach art and design. If you are lucky enough to be near one, check out their website. Find the classes teaching what you want and enroll. If you are not inclined to actually learn the décor skills, find a student there who needs to create a project for school credit. Sometimes it might be free, or simply the cost of raw materials. If there is a fee, you can often bargain with the student. You'll still pay only a fraction of what he or she will charge in a few years, and you both win. Ask the teachers who the gifted students are, and then see if you can arrange for one to help you.

"Have nothing in your home that you don't know to be useful or believe to be beautiful." –William Morris

So remember to surround yourself with great things and at great prices. And when you're decorating, don't just think Feng Shui –

think *How to Live Like a MILLIONAIRE When You're a Million Short!*

Chap Wrap 'n Recap

- Charity and Thrift Shops
- Yard and Estate Sales
- Swap and Prop Shops
- Rental Houses and Hotel Outlets
- Consignment and Used Furniture
- Buy it. Use it. Sell it.
- Find It. Fix It. Keep It.
- DIY and How-to Videos
- Unusual Can Be Chic
- Art Schools and Students

Feathering Your Nest with the Best Quiz – True or False

1. When you look at used couches, check under the pillows for coins.
2. When you buy old paintings, check to see if they're signed by Renoir.
3. On YouTube, you can learn how to build a chest or build muscles on your chest.
4. DIY means Don't Imitate Yodelers.
5. Never ever believe you can get something good from Craigslist.

8. Home Sweet MILLIONAIRE'S Home

How would you like to live in a two-story, three-bedroom, three-bathroom apartment, with two living rooms, one sunken from the other, a marble staircase, and a black Italian marble bath and shower, all in a ritzy area of Los Angeles – for FREE? Or better still, be PAID to live there? I did. And I was.

Or how would you like to live in a beautiful four-bedroom house with a swimming pool . . . in Bel Air, another upscale area of Los Angeles . . . and be PAID to live *there*? My girlfriend Lisa does . . . and is.

Or in Manhattan, how would you like to have a 3,000 square foot loft apartment in a hip area of the city – and live there for 30 years – for FREE?! My friend Paul did.

There's No Place Like *Someone Else's Luxury* Home

When I first moved to Los Angeles, I didn't know anyone. Not a soul. I didn't know where I wanted to live . . . or where I could *afford* to live. But one night I was in a bar and met a real estate broker. He told me he had an opportunity for me where I could live rent-free – and no, I didn't have to trade any favors for it! He had a client who needed someone to "take care of" his newly bought apartment building. And too bad, the only apartment that was vacant for me to move into . . . was the one the previous owner had moved out of! The gorgeous two-story-two-living-roomed-marble-bathroomed-mini-palace. I accepted the offer and promptly settled into my first home in Los Angeles.

Not only didn't I pay rent, but the new owner of the building *paid me* $500 per month to live there! All I had to do was watch the property and collect rents from 12 other residents who lived in the other apartments. Since the owner was out of the country a lot, I also had to drive his new Mercedes convertible regularly to keep it in good order, so I even had a hot car. It was a really tough time in my life! Duh, not really. It was a blast.

The apartment was so huge and beautiful, I was frequently asked by people if they could hold parties or art openings there – and they would have paid me for that, too. I didn't take them up on it. But for a year, I lived in this absolute showplace – and was *paid* for the privilege. I ended up writing my first screenplay while I was living there.

Of course, it was total luck that I ran into this real estate broker, but I was open to the situation when it was offered, and it ended up being fantastic. I even "inherited" some of the furniture and artwork that the old owner left. I still have a huge painting that was on the wall, and I always wonder if it might have been painted by some famous artist and is somehow worth a fortune. Unfortunately, it's not signed, so I've never found out.

After a year I had to move when they knocked down the building, since the new owner had bought the property in order to sell the land for a much bigger condo complex. But for that lovely year, I was able to call it my happy home.

"A girl phoned me the other day and said . . . 'Come on over, there's nobody home.' I went over. Nobody was home." –Rodney Dangerfield

Their Home is Where *Her* Heart Is

My friend Lisa also got her living situation in Bel Air sort of by accident. Someone was looking for a dog-sitter while they were away on vacation for several months. A friend knew Lisa loved dogs, so they told her about it, and she became the rich couple's regular house-sitter while they were away . . . every summer for eight years! Even when the dog was gone, they still paid her to watch their home while they went on extended summer vacations.

A Lofty Way to Live in New York

My friend Paul had a different set of circumstances. We all know how expensive it is to live in Manhattan. And many of the apartments are small, especially affordable ones. But a few weeks after Paul moved into a loft, the owner of the property died. His relatives who inherited it didn't take proper steps with the building, so all the residents there went on a rent strike. They literally didn't pay rent for 30 years! Finally, after decades, the family got their sh*t together – and started charging him (and the other tenants) $1,000 a month. In Manhattan! And they didn't have to pay back rent, either. Just recently Paul sold his "rights" to the place. As an incentive for him to move, they gave him enough money to buy a house – *Yowzaa!*

Now all these stories started with happenstance . . . or luck. That's true. But lucky for you, there are other ways to find situations like these, where you don't need luck, you just need the Internet.

Hop on Over to My House-Sit!

There are numerous sites that match house sitters and pet sitters with home owners. The reasons are various. Some owners need someone to take care of their pets while they are gone. Others just want the house not to be vacant. They might want their mail to be collected, their plants to be watered, or in the winter, to have the snow cleared.

> "I long, as does every human being, to be at home wherever I find myself." –Maya Angelou

House-sitters are finding places in all different areas of the U.S. and Canada as well as opportunities in foreign countries, too. Here are a few sites that offer housesitting or pet sitting opportunities. Depending on the site, it's from $25 to $55 to sign up for a year, and then you can check the site for places you may want to housesit or pet sit.

www.TrustedHousesitters.com

www.HouseSitter.com

www.LuxuryHousesitting.com

www.HousesittersAmerica.com

www.MindMyHouse.com

www.Housecarers.com

www.care.com/house-sitting-jobs

www.rover.com/become-a-sitter/

www.caretaker.org

Some of these may be longer assignments, and some just for vacations. Some will be regular houses or apartments; others may be mansions or estates. The point is that there are many kinds of situations available, and some people take advantage of these possibilities to travel and see different parts of the world . . . for free. They can live like the locals, without having to pay hotel bills or even rent of any kind. Sometimes it's just rent-free; and sometimes, the house-sitters get paid as well.

"Where thou art, that is home." –Emily Dickinson

A Man's Home is *Someone Else's* Castle

My friend John was an expert at getting free housing, and sometimes getting paid to stay in luxury. He lived rent-free for more than seven years in some of the best areas of Southern California.

He didn't go through the Internet, but developed his own personal way to find great living situations. He found that for animal lovers, pet sitting is a great way to get housing and maybe get paid, too.

Changing careers at midlife is becoming very common these days. Like many baby boomers, John made a change from a successful career and had to start over, so his money wasn't flowing like it was before. He had to take more risks when he was starting his new life, so he decided to begin pet sitting and housesitting to cut his expenses.

At first, he put the word out to friends that he would pet-sit for free. He started getting gigs. First, for some cute pugs; then, for a shy German shepherd; then, for numerous other pampered pooches. After getting some good testimonials extolling his animal magnetism, John got his first paying gig. And from then on, he got paid to sit. He got money to live and places to live, too.

As friends heard about what he was doing, they started finding him *long-term sitting gigs*, most of which didn't pay, but they did allow him to live rent free for the next four years!

When that period ended, he made up business cards at Vistaprint and dropped them off at veterinarians' offices in or near wealthy neighborhoods. Sometimes, he baked cookies and dropped them off at the vets to entice them to remember him when one of their clients needed a sitter. It worked. Word of mouth, business cards, and cookies were the best investments he made – so that he could live like a millionaire . . . even though he was a million short.

If the idea of housesitting or pet sitting appeals to you, spread the word and let people know you are interested, or check the online sites. Who knows? You could end up living in the lap of luxury for free . . . or even getting paid for it.

> **"I live on a one-way street that's also a dead end. I'm not sure how I got there." – Steven Wright**

I've even heard that some real estate companies that handle mansions and estates don't like them to look empty for potential buyers, so they sometimes have people reside there so the places look lived in. I don't personally know anyone who's done it – but if you know any mansions or estates that need a house-sitter, you can tell them I'm available!

Being a **resident manager** can also be a way to get free rent. You'll have to work for it, but the amount and times vary. Sometimes, if you're lucky, it can be for a small building where you don't have to do much – and possibly even in a luxury building. These may be hard to find, but someone has to do it . . . so why not YOU? I found it, and I wasn't even looking! Many people get free rent being apartment managers for more modest buildings, and that's certainly a way to save money as well. It all depends on where you want to live and how much work you want to do for it.

If You're Broke, Don't Be Gloomy – Get a Rich Roomie!

Living in Los Angeles, I know how paying rent can suck up your entire paycheck. That's "if" you get one. There are so many actors, writers, and wannabes here, and a lot of the time they don't have regular jobs. Not only is it hard to *pay* for an apartment, sometimes it's hard to get approved for one, because your credit rating sucks. And rents have gone up so astronomically you almost have to *be* a millionaire to live anywhere here on your own. In any case, many individuals choose to go the roommate route.

I say, why get a roommate who has the same money issues that you do? Instead, find a roommate who lives in a sprawling Beverly Hills house but doesn't want to live alone. Maybe a divorcee or empty nester who isn't used to being all by herself or himself in that big beautiful place! I knew a gal who lived in a magnificent Bel Air estate with the woman who owned it. The young actress found out about it through a friend of a friend. The older woman's children were grown and out of the house, and her husband had recently died. She didn't want to move, but she felt too isolated and lonely by herself. So she was over-the-moon happy to have the younger gal move in and share her spacious surroundings. She charged her rent, but very little, since she didn't really need the money; she just wanted the company. The aspiring actress who moved in had the run of the place, and the woman even helped her practice her lines when she went on auditions!

> "When I got to Dallas, I was struggling – sleeping on the floor with six guys in a three-bedroom apartment. I used to drive around, look at the big houses, and imagine what it would be like to live there, and use that as motivation." –Mark Cuban

Of course, in any roommate situation, it all depends on "who" you're sharing the space with and how you get along. Whether they're rich or poor, make sure you know what they want in a roommate and that you agree on what your boundaries will be. One of my friends owns a big house and has three roommates who pay rent to help him with his mortgage. Don runs a home-based catering business, so he won't let his tenants use the kitchen. That works for them, but I doubt most people would want to live in a place where they weren't allowed to cook. There are all kinds of different situations with roommates, so make sure it's someone you can live with – it's a real pain to have to keep moving all the time . . . that is, unless it's to house-sit at somebody's mansion!

You can find roommates the same way you look for an apartment – on Craigslist, at apartment services or roommate services. If you want to be a rich person's roomie, look in the affluent neighborhoods. You may find that you don't have to pay as much rent as you'd think.

> "I told my mother-in-law that my house was her house, and she said, 'Get the hell off my property.'" –Joan Rivers

A Home Away from Home

But let's say you don't want to live in someone else's home. You want your own luxury place – but at a less-than-luxury price.

Many people have found that living in a foreign country can be lush and lavish – and cost very little. There are many countries where you can literally live like a millionaire for a fraction of the price it costs to live in the U.S., even in a not-so-great place.

A friend of mine lived in a four-bedroom villa on the coast of La Serena, Chile. It was right on the beach, and he paid next-to-nothing in rent.

> **"I installed a skylight in my apartment . . . the people who live above me are furious!"** –Steven Wright

If you're partial to California weather and beaches, but not the price they cost, there's actually a little secret just a skip and a jump away. Many expats are taking advantage of the cost of living just south of the border in Mexico.

There are various communities there where expats from around the world are living for 25 to 35 percent of the cost of living in Southern California. I have a writer friend who lives there and loves it.

He indicates that you can get a satellite box from the U.S. and pick up all the American programming. When you get a VPN, a Virtual Private Network, your computer will think it is in the U.S. Depending on where you are, you can make a quick trip over the border to shop or enjoy the U.S. benefits first hand. And with the peso going down compared to the U.S. dollar, it's getting cheaper as costs are rising in the U.S.

Many people worldwide retire there for this reason. And to add to the good life, he says it's actually safer there than in the U.S. So consider retiring like a millionaire, too. He says you can live in a luxurious beach house in Mexico for less than $1,000 per month.

"I am a marvelous housekeeper. Every time I leave a man I keep his house." –Zsa Zsa Gabor

If you want to go farther away, there are many other countries that offer wonderful living for less, and some have become havens for retirees.

A recent article in Bankrate.com lists six of the cheapest places to retire, including Chiang Mai, Thailand, Guam, and Valencia, Spain.

Chiang Mai is known to be cheap even by Thailand's standards. A 1,200 square foot condo might cost as little as $450 to $500 per month. Combine that with great weather and a low cost of living, and it might make you feel like a merry millionaire.

Guam, situated 3,700 miles southwest of Honolulu, is a lower-cost alternative to Hawaii that shares the same climate. One-bedroom apartments in Guam can rent for as low as $400 per month, with luxury units facing the sea costing $1,000 per month.

In Valencia, Spain, a two-bedroom apartment rents for about $780 a month.

These places could be very desirable for a retiree on a fixed income or just someone wanting to live the good life for less.

You can read more at:

http://www.bankrate.com/finance/retirement/6-cheap-places-retire-abroad.aspx

Author Tim Leffel discusses not only where you can live inexpensively, but where you can travel for vacation on the cheap as well:

www.CheapestDestinationsblog.com

You Can Never Go Home Again . . . But You Can Live Abroad!

I haven't lived abroad myself, so I'm not an expert at this, but check online and you'll find many sites and resources to give you information.

International Living publishes a new Annual Global Retirement Index every year listing the best places to retire:

> https://internationalliving.com/2016/01/the-best-places-to-retire-2016/

When looking at possible places to live abroad, be sure to take into account not only what you'll be paying for rent, but the general conditions of the country, the costs of living there, and the medical facilities and costs in case you get sick.

Try Home Shopping by Going Swapping

www.Goswap.org is a site that offers permanent house swapping and real estate exchange: You can trade homes, land, boats, cars, RVs, even airplanes. They list properties in the U.S. and in various countries all over the world.

Chap Wrap 'n Recap

- Get Lucky
- House-Sitting and Pet-Sitting
- Be a Resident Manager
- Find a Rich Roomie
- Live Abroad

How to *Really* Live in a MILLIONAIRE'S Home Quiz – True or False

1. If you want to live in a fancy house, break into one that's for sale and become a squatter.

2. In New York, if you want to find a great apartment, look through the obituaries and put a bid on the place before anyone else knows it's available.

3. If you want to house-sit, you have to have a sitter's license.

4. Apartment managers have to work their asses off the whole damn week and weekends, too.

5. If you're pet sitting for someone with a dog, you have to supply your own pooper scoopers.

9. Giving, Getting, and Gala-vanting

"No one has ever become poor by giving." –Anne Frank, *The Diary of Anne Frank*

Charity Begins at Home

Picture yourself getting a Swedish massage once a day, a facial every other day, eating fabulous gourmet food, taking classes, and staying four sumptuous nights at a luxurious resort and spa, then coming home ultra-relaxed, super-refreshed, and an amazing ten pounds thinner? OMG – who wouldn't want to do this? But alas, such is only for those living the life of the rich and/or famous. Wow, it sounds like the Housewives of Beverly Hills. Or the Millionaire Men of Malibu! Or . . . Me? You said it! I did it! And here's how!

Giving Myself Away!

I had a wealthy girlfriend who used to always go to fabulous spots around the world. She'd frequently tell me about one of her favorite places, Canyon Ranch Spa in Tucson, Arizona. It's a luxury resort and spa where you get lavish accommodations and healthy gourmet meals, along with fitness classes, massages and beauty treatments, all as part of a package. Angie used to go there at least twice a year, sometimes more. A four-night package cost about $4,000. (And that's just for the "smaller" room, not the deluxe!) OMG – Could I afford it? Never! Was I jealous? Always. At that time, my idea of a resort and spa was going to the $39 a month gym and going home afterwards to take a bubble bath with a $1.59 loofa! But I could dream, couldn't I?

Still, I always kept it in the back of my mind, that one day, when I got rich, I would treat myself to Canyon Ranch Spa. Needless to say, I didn't get rich. But . . .

One day, a girlfriend called me to say she was working with The American Lung Association and they were going to be staging a Bachelorette Auction. Since I was single, would I want to be "auctioned off" as a bachelorette for a night on the town? The money they raised would go to the charity.

I have always been adventurous, so I said, "Sure." It sounded like fun – having lots of handsome strangers (hopefully, they'd be handsome!) bid lots of money to go out on a date with me.

Once I agreed, my friend gave me more details on what I would have to do before the event. Each of the bachelorettes had to plan their own special evening for the bidders, and get things donated for the date. Some of the women were able to get restaurants to donate a dinner-for-two. One woman arranged a round of golf at a country club, with lunch at the clubhouse afterwards; another gal arranged dinner at a bistro and theater tickets to a local play.

I thought about it and realized, "This is my chance to go to Canyon Ranch Spa!" I called the management of the resort and explained that I was working with The American Lung Association, and we were looking for donations for the Bachelorette Auction. If the resort would donate a four-day package (in fact, two separate ones, since my date and I had to have separate rooms,) they would get a page in the event program, a mention in all the publicity, and it would all be tax deductible for them.

Guess what – they were all too happy to do it! So I had gotten my package to Canyon Ranch Spa. Not only that, but I approached an airline for two round-trip tickets to Tucson – and got them; and a limo company donated a stretch limo for a few hours to take us to the airport!

The night of the auction, when I was being bid on, I knew I was going to Canyon Ranch Spa. I just didn't know yet . . . with whom! In fact, I actually brought a shill. One of my guy friends wanted to go to Canyon Ranch, and he knew that the date package would probably go for much less than it was worth. So he came to the auction to bid on me. But as the bidding went on, there was a very handsome stranger – hubba, hubba – who was bidding against him. I started shaking my head to signal my friend . . . "No, don't go any higher! Please, stop bidding!" So what happened?

The handsome guy WON the date with me. Btw, he *also* got a terrific bargain. A trip that was worth over $4000 for one – and with the two of us it was worth $8000. My mysterious stranger ended up buying it for only $1000. Not to mention, getting a date with a million-dollar gal . . . i.e. ME!

The day of the trip, he arrived in the limo, and he even brought me flowers. It was a terrific time. We each had our own rooms, too. As it turned out, we were "not" a romantic pair, but we both had a grand time at Canyon Ranch Spa – me totally comped – and the handsome stranger, for only a *fraction* of what it would normally cost. As for how I liked my mini-vacation at Canyon Ranch Spa? Just call me the totally relaxed, mega-massaged, healthy, faux-wealthy, Marilyn of Marina Del Rey!

What YOU Can Do – Volunteer!

Okay, let's face it – not everyone is going to have the chance to be in a bachelorette auction! And even if they did, most people wouldn't want to parade down a runway and be ogled and bid on by strangers. Only a crazy lady like me would jump at the chance to do that!

But take heart! The wonderful thing about volunteering for charities is that there are all kinds of them, and lots of different ways to help. Volunteering for your favorite charity is something everyone can do. Almost every city has organizations that put on events to raise funds for worthy causes. Check out some in your city, and call them to see how you can sign up to help.

> "You give but little when you give of your possessions. It is when you give of yourself that your truly give." – Kahlil Gibran, *The Prophet*

Starry, Star-Filled Nights

In order to raise needed funds, many charities plan gala evenings that charge pricey fees for their tickets. Sometimes, these tickets might cost $100 each, or $200, sometimes even $500 to $1000. If you assist in planning the event or help out that night, volunteers often get to go to the actual event for free. You might help with the invitations or with calling people; you might help put up decorations, or fill up gift bags, or do any kind of pre-event preparations. In the process, you will meet all kinds of new people and make new friends. Some of them may even BE millionaires. (That is, if you are looking for a date or mate.) Wealthy people have favorite causes, and often donate their time as well as their money. In any case, you'll get to meet others who believe in helping the same kinds of causes that you do. In addition, working on the event in advance, you can find out about some of the things going on that evening. Not to mention, you'll get a chance to wear those incredibly stunning designer dresses you got on the cheap from reading the fashion chapter here!

> **"I'm a true believer in karma. You get what you give, whether it's bad or good." – Sandra Bullock**

Silence is Golden . . . Perhaps for YOU!

What are some of the ways you can "cash in" from volunteering for the event? One example is that lots of charities hold **silent auctions** at their events. Only, this time, YOU won't be the item they are bidding on! Silent auctions might feature donated gifts like hotel packages, massages, jewelry, art, dinners at different restaurants, even a walk-on part in a TV Show. Not only that – but if you help to acquire some of the gifts or services for their auctions, you will know how much they are worth – and can bid on them the night of the affair. Many times, items or services go for THOUSANDS less than they are worth. Also, when you leave, charity events often give away gift bags . . . otherwise, known as **swag bags**. These have all kinds of cool things in them – from cosmetics to books to jewelry to t-shirts – as well as discount certificates for expensive stores, spas or salons. You can keep them yourself or give them away as gifts.

> **"That's why charity work is very selfish at the same time, because it makes you feel good." –Maria Menounos**

How I Bid It . . . To Win It!

The gym that I used to go to years ago, Sports Club LA, charged new members a $1,200 initiation fee to join, and then $175/month. Add that up for the first year, and it came to $3,290. Those prices were definitely for a millionaire, or at least big spenders, but not someone like me with no income at the time. However, I was at a charity event for the Venice Family Clinic and was browsing through the silent auction area. I saw a listing for "A Year's Membership at the Sports Club LA." The bidding started at $250. Now, $250 may seem like a lot of money to plunk down, especially if you're just volunteering to get into the event for free. But I knew that for this particular gym, it was a real deal. So I waited until near the end of the silent auction. Only two people had bid on the SCLA gym membership. It was up to $300. So I bid $350 and won it. I got a membership I knew was valued at $3290 . . . for just $350! Savings: $2,940. Plus, I got the added benefits of going to the coolest gym in town and meeting all the other members who could afford to pay their fees. What's more, it contributed to my health and well-being. And, oh yeah, I also met my boyfriend of 14 years there! Not bad for $350.

> "It's not just about being able to write a check. It's being able to touch somebody's life." –Oprah Winfrey

Sold to the Highest Bidder . . . But YOU Still Win!

There are sometimes regular auctions at charity events as well. I was at one where Sharon Stone was the auctioneer. There were many famous stars, interesting celebs, and VIPs at the event, and we all had lots of fun watching as she announced the many fabulous things up for auction. There were expensive jewelry items, object's d'art, dinners for a party of eight, cooked by a famous chef at your house, a walk-on role in a TV series, and Sharon even auctioned off the dress she was wearing! Although she didn't take it off then and there. (*That* probably would have gone for much more!) It was fascinating to watch and see who were the rich folks who bid on these expensive items – and how they kept going higher and higher if they really wanted to be the winning bidder. Sharon is apparently a recurring auctioneer goddess for amfAR Cinema Against AIDS Gala, and she has talked about many of the crazy things she's auctioned off.

I read an article by Bryan Alexander in *USA Today* in which Sharon was quoted as saying: "One year, Calvin Klein was in the audience, and I said, 'Who'll pay $5,000 to see if Calvin Klein is wearing Calvin Klein underwear?' And the bidding went crazy. So I said, 'Calvin, drop your drawers!' He stood up, and he was wearing Calvins."

The fun part is that if you volunteer for a charity that has these star-studded events, you may get to go and not only see a celebrity auctioneer, but also all the snazzy Hollywood actors and VIPs who attend.

> **"I profoundly feel that the art of living is the art of giving. You're fulfilled in the moment of giving, of doing something beyond yourself." –Laurance Rockefeller**

When You Give . . . You Get!

So now you realize that by giving, you will definitely receive. The very act of giving makes you feel good. Plus, when you volunteer, you'll be meeting new people and making new friends, some of whom may even BE millionaires. As I've indicated, the volunteers for charities often get to go to their events for free, even the extremely expensive ones you wouldn't be able to afford on your own. Say you get comped to go to a $1000 event. Nice, huh? And once there, you can schmooze with the wealthy folks; meet a millionaire; or bid on the silent auction items, etc. In addition to fancy galas or auctions, there might be barbecues, picnics, casino nights, walkathons, carnivals, seminars, or all kinds of other possible events or activities. The important thing is you will be giving to a worthy cause and helping others – and that alone should make you *feel* like a millionaire. It's a win-win situation – so volunteer, and enjoy it all.

"The only gift is a portion of thyself." –Ralph Waldo Emerson

What's YOUR Favorite Charity?

There are many different types of charities, and you can choose to volunteer with one that fits your specific interests and passions. Check the Internet to find one near you that you might want to work with – or that has events where you could volunteer and enjoy yourself at the same time. The best part is you'll not only be giving to a cause you believe in, but you'll be meeting others, both volunteers and attendees, who are interested in the same field or arena. Here are some of the kinds of charities you may want to check out:

Are You an Animal Lover?

There are various kinds of **Animal Charities** with missions to help animals in different ways. These include: Wildlife conservation organizations; Pet and Animal Welfare & Rescue Organizations; Hunting & Fishing Conservation Groups; and Zoos and Aquariums.

For Eco-Minded Peeps

Environmental Charities include those for Environmental Conservation & Protection, or for Parks and Nature Centers.

Healthy 'n Hearty

Maybe you're not a doctor and can't research or cure diseases, but a way that you can help fight illnesses is by volunteering for different kinds of **Health Charities.** These could include Disease & Disorder Charities; Medical Services & Treatment Charities; Medical Research Charities; and Patient and Family Support Charities.

Are You Yearning for Learning?

Educational Charities include Private Elementary, Jr. High, and High Schools; Universities and Colleges; Scholarship and financial aid services; School Reform and Experimental Education; and Support for students, teachers, and parents.

Near and Dear to My ARTS

Arts and Culture Charities celebrate the arts and our cultural heritage, and include organizations such as Museums & Art Galleries; Performing Arts; Libraries & Historical Societies; and Public Broadcasting and Media.

Helping Near and Faraway

International NGOs (Non-governmental organizations) are charities that may be based here but provide help to other countries, such as International Development NGOs; Disaster Relief & Humanitarian NGOs; Peace & Human Rights NGOs; Conservation NGOs; or Child Sponsorship Organizations.

> "If you haven't got any charity in your heart, you have the worst kind of heart trouble." –Bob Hope

With regard to international giving, there are also many ways to volunteer abroad, some of which are mentioned in the travel chapter, "Getaways and Globetrotting Galore." And don't forget, when you have clothes, furniture or household items you no longer want, it's great to donate them to your favorite local charity.

Chap Wrap 'n Recap

- Giving Begets Getting
- Look for Charities in Your City
- Volunteer for Your Favorite Causes
- Make New Friends While You Help Others
- Check Out Silent Auctions
- Different Kinds of Charities

The Giving, Getting, and Gala-vanting Quiz – True or False

1. If you volunteer at a charity gala, everyone will know you are really poor.
2. If you bid in a silent auction and don't pay up, they cut off your ears.
3. The "SWAG" in swag bags was named for Stars Who Are Greedy.

4. Auction items always cost more than if you bought them retail.
5. Items sold for charity have microchips so you can't return them to stores.
6. Volunteering for a charity event is a win-win-win!

"Those who are happiest are those who do the most for others." –Booker T. Washington

10. Celebrations, Elations, and Festifications

"The more you praise and celebrate your life, the more there is in life to celebrate." –Oprah Winfrey

Birthday Bonanzas

Birthdays can be traumatic. Admitting to all your friends that you're another year older . . . eeek! Or worse, not having any friends who care enough to remember. What if there's no one to give you a party? What if there's no one to come to your party? What if you have no money to throw a party?

No worries. I'm going to give you a bunch of ideas and ways to celebrate your birthday and other holidays, too – without having to spend a bundle . . . or anything at all.

On your special day, I wish you peace, love, fun . . . and lots of expensive things that don't cost a penny.

First, my confession: Every year I have my *Annual 35th Birthday Bash*. I've had it for years, although I won't tell you for how many.

I invite just about everyone I know to come to my annual event at a nice restaurant. Everyone laughs when they get the invitation, since I never "age" at all. It's always my *35th*. The famous comedian Jack Benny used to celebrate his 39th every year.

"Age is strictly a case of mind over matter. If you don't mind, it doesn't matter" –Jack Benny

Wow. Inviting gobs of people to come to a restaurant? How can I afford it? Easy.

It's a buy-your-own-dinner event. I pick a restaurant that has lots of space or a big backroom. The eatery has to agree to let everyone pay by separate checks. Then I can have ten or twenty or forty or even sixty people. It assures me I won't be lonely on my birthday. And I don't have to blindly hope that someone will invite me out on my big day.

Everyone always has the best time. One year I held it at a Chinese restaurant. One time at a Mexican place, once at a bistro that gave us a back room with its own bar, bartender, and happy hour prices all night long for all the drinks and food. That year, I even showed nine episodes of my new *Never Kiss a Frog* Web Series on their big screen TVs around the room.

Another year I found a place with a four-man soul band, the members of which were about 80 to 90 years old. They were amazing. After dinner, when two police officers showed up, I thought they were *male strippers* hired by one of my friends. But no, these guys weren't taking their clothes off – they were real cops!

It turns out the restaurant didn't have a license for "live music," and the police officers wanted to stop the band from playing.

Since the musicians were well into their eighties, the guests and I pleaded with the officers, saying it wasn't really "live" music – these oldsters were almost "dead" – so please, let them keep playing and don't haul them away in handcuffs!

Even the policemen couldn't keep straight faces, realizing that this little blues spot without a "live" music license was itself a "dying" spot. So instead of arresting the band, the officers settled for a piece of cake (we didn't have donuts) and then they left, whereupon the geriatric musicians happily resumed playing.

"Time and tide wait for no man, but time always stands still for a woman of thirty."–Robert Frost

Another time I picked a restaurant by the beach that had a 13-piece brass band on Wednesday nights in their back room. Unfortunately for the restaurant, but fortunately for me – no one knew about the band yet, so no one came to hear them. Except all my party guests! They thought I had hired the band just for my birthday. It was an amazing blues group, The Blowin' Smoke Rhythm & Blues Band, featuring the fabulous Smokettes.

It was phenomenal. First, we all ate and shared fun and conversation out by the water; then we headed to the back room for our own private dance party. My friends didn't stop talking about it for months. Oh, and the restaurant later became a real hotspot, known for their great Wednesday Night Band Fests.

Btw, my parents were there for a couple of my parties, and I trained them well; they told everyone they couldn't *remember* how old I was! My boyfriend also got into the spirit of the parties. For the seven parties (and seven years) he lasted, he used to make up funny t-shirts for people. One of my friends says he still has all seven shirts. After my boyfriend and I got the "seven year itch" and split up – no more t-shirts for guests.

Even without the free t-shirts, people like my birthday parties so much they've asked me to have them more than once a year!

201

"I believe in loyalty. When a woman reaches an age she likes, she should stick with it." –Eva Gabor

On one of my recent annual 35th birthdays, I found a dress shop that offered to hold the party for me in their store. What's more, they would provide the wine and snacks if I brought at least six new women to the shop. Not only that, but they would allow the birthday girl (in this case, *moi*) – to pick out a dress or item that was priced at $100 or less for FREE.

This store also sold high-end sex toys, and for my party they had the owner of that company come in and give us a demonstration of all the vibrators, lotions, and potions. It was a hoot! (No, she didn't strip, or display her vajayjay! She just gave a talk and showed the items.)

It was a win-win situation, because the store got to meet new customers; my girlfriends and I got to try on clothes (and bought some); the store made sales, and everyone had a ball.

It didn't cost me anything to have the party, but it was a fun and fab event for everyone who attended. Oh, and the woman who sold the sex toys got quite a few new clients as well. Not to mention, the women's husbands or boyfriends had fun later that night, too!

"Let them eat cake!" –Marie Antoinette

For every 35th birthday party every year, I usually get a cake and design it myself. I bring that, but otherwise everyone buys their own food and picks what they want to eat. This year the cake had black icing (it was designed like a Hollywood clapboard) and everyone ended up with black tongues. We all had tons of laughs and posted lots of black tongues sticking out on our Facebook pages. Of course, the main rule is and always has been – no one can know how old I am!

"Age is a number, and yours is unlisted." –Unknown

Some of the fun at all of these parties includes going around the tables and having everyone introduce themselves. People will tell how they know me or how we met. They can do "roasts" or games. No matter what, it's always a grand time. Once, one of my friends made everyone guess "How does Marilyn live?" Everyone made up stories about how I made money in secret ways. Everything from working for the CIA to being a proof reader for a Chinese fortune cookie company. I don't do either of these, but I do manage to live like a millionaire.

Okay, so now you know: you can plan a wonderful birthday party for yourself (or your loved one) – and not have it cost you anything. In addition, you'll probably receive gobs of gifts from guests, too. And have plenty of fun and laughs.

"Birthdays are good for you. Statistics show that the people who have the most live the longest." –Father Larry Lorenzi.

To reiterate, the guests never mind that it's a buy-your-own-meal event, because they can order exactly what they want and pay what they want. I'll probably be the only one in the world to have a buy-your-own-dinner funeral. Only for that, I'd rather NOT be the guest of honor!

One other thing to remember for your Annual Birthday Bash - whatever "age" you choose to be: *You don't have to have your party on your actual birthday.*

In fact, I recommend that you don't. Why? Because there are many places that will give you a *free meal* on the *day* of your birthday . . . and you want to be able to take advantage of that. In fact, you can probably find places to have both lunch and dinner free on your special day. Not to mention, lots of other possible free goodies, too.

Whenever you go to a restaurant you like, sign up for their email list. Almost all of them will ask you the date of your birthday. And most of them will email you a coupon or offer for something free on your birthday – often a free entrée. Lots of restaurants will offer you a free meal just on the actual day of your birthday, while others make the offer available any time during the month, or within a few weeks of the actual day.

This means you're going to go to a couple of restaurants on the actual day of your birthday – and other restaurants at other times during the month – to get a free birthday meal. Birthdays should always last a whole month, don't you think? I do. Especially since I never get any older!

Other Places for Birthday Specials

There are so many places that offer birthday gifts for celebrating your day or month. That's why it's good to sign up for restaurant or store mailings wherever you go. They may offer discounts during the year, but for your birthday you might get a special discount or freebie. This is not only for restaurants, but for many retail stores and all kinds of activities as well.

Some places that offer birthday discounts and freebies include: Hardware stores, comedy clubs, baseball games, beauty salons, beauty product retailers, and even Kmart. The state of Missouri even gives you a free lottery ticket! Petco offers a free treat for your pet. Except I'm not sure if it's for your pet's birthday or for yours.

One fabulous offer in Southern California is for the beautiful island of Catalina. On the day of your birthday, you can get a FREE BOAT RIDE TO CATALINA! (Plus lots of freebies when you get there.) This is no small thing. The boat trip usually costs around $38 one way or $76 round trip. So it's definitely cool to go for free. Usually, you can find a loved one or friend who wants to go, and they will pay their own fare, or if you're feeling generous, you can split it.

I have a girlfriend who goes to Catalina every year on her birthday. She goes alone, but meets lots of other people who have her same birthday. They actually have reunions every year on the boat, discussing what's happened for them during the past year, and having loads of fun and laughs in the process.

Then, when they get to the island, there are a bunch of activities that are also free for birthday guys and gals.

Once in Catalina, you can get FREE PARASAILING, (if you're brave enough – woweeee!) and a FREE CART RENTAL to ride around the island. There are also oodles of freebies at the restaurants there. It's a delightful place to go on your big day.

http://ecatalina.com/catalina-birthday-specials

Wherever you are, whether at home or traveling, if it's your birthday month, check to see where they'll make you feel extra special.

www.heyitsfree.net/birthday-freebies

Columbia Sportswear Company offers a 20 percent discount when you sign up on their birthday list. CVS Pharmacy gives you an extra $3 to spend.

DSW (Discount Shoe Warehouse) offers you a $5 gift Certificate when you sign up on their list. World Market offers a $10 or 10 percent off coupon on their Rewards program.

> **"Put yourself in a state of mind where you say to yourself, "Here is an opportunity for you to celebrate like never before, my own power, my own ability to get myself to do whatever is necessary." –Tony Robbins**

If you like bowling, AMF offers a $20 Certificate for your bowling party. Just about any restaurant or retail business offers some sort of a discount. So check your favorite place before you go or even once you get there. Bring your smartphone and you can sign up instantly.

I often shop at Chico's for clothes, and they always send me a $10 discount coupon for my birthday, as does White House Black Market.

Remember to sign up at the stores you patronize, and most of the time, you'll get a special bonus for your special day.

You know how they have Wedding Gift Registries in stores? Why don't they have Birthday Gift Registries? That way, you could get gifts you really want. This has actually been handled on Amazon and some other sites by having a section for your wish list! My boyfriend and I even talked about where we'd have our Wedding Registry. We love to eat out and travel, so we'd tell friends we've registered at Groupon!

Other Freebies-On-Your-Birthday Sites:

www.freebie-depot.com/birthday-freebie-list

www.dealnews.com/features/Free-Presents-The-Best-Retail-Restaurant-Birthday-Freebies/1081056.html

So celebrate your birthday! Eat for free all day long, find countless fun things to do, and even get some presents for yourself!

> The way I see it, you should live every day like it's your birthday. —Paris Hilton

So You're Getting Hitched! (Or Celebrating Another Year of Marital Misery!)

For really special events like getting married, many businesses will give you something extra. If you are flying to your honeymoon destination, mention it to the aircrew when boarding, and they might comp you with champagne or other goodies.

Even if you're married a long time, you still might be eligible for some perks. It's not as usual for restaurants to have anniversary promotions as birthday offers, but sometimes, when signing up, they ask you the date of your anniversary. Who's to say if you're married or not? Pick any date you like, say it's your *anni,* and just take a friend. Unlike a birthday, you won't have to produce your driver's license to prove it. In fact, make every day of 365 days your anniversary. Just be sure to go to a different restaurant each time.

> "Take my wife . . . please!" –Henny Youngman

For your anniversary, or for other occasions like graduations, bar mitzvahs, or quinceaneras, check to see if the restaurant offers anything. Drop a hint to the waiter or hostess. Even if it's not company policy, the manager might give you a glass of wine or a piece of cake with a candle in it. And some places will send a bunch of waiters over to sing to you. But you should go, anyway!

"It's a Piece of Cake" Snippet

You may want to be sure you and your dining guests are all in sync. I went to dinner with a few of my relatives to celebrate a belated birthday for my cute little 10-year-old cousin who I hadn't seen for several months. I whispered to the waiter that it was Amanda's birthday. They brought over a humongous slice of cake with a candle in it, and started to sing. At which point, Amanda yelled out . . . "It's not my birthday!"

The waiter was a good sport and laughed, but it was a little awkward. Especially when Amanda's rambunctious 12-year-old brother, turned to her and yelled, "Shut up, so we can eat cake."

Also, it's not just *your* birthday or anniversary that counts. Sometimes the business will have an anniversary or the owner has a birthday and offers a special discount for the customers. Car dealers frequently advertise specials on their anniversary. My friend John told me there's a Toastmaster's group that meets at a Mercedes dealer, and on the dealership's anniversary, each member gets 10 percent off a car. Meaning if someone buys a car on that day, they get an extra discount. No, it's not like one person gets a steering wheel and another one gets a hubcap!

Other Peoples' Birthdays

Giving, Gifting and Regifting

You can't have a chapter on birthdays and not talk about gifts. So what do you do if you get invited to a party, but you're broke?

Other chapters deal with shopping, buying clothes, being a foodie, traveling, etc. – and you can certainly "gift" people with any of the ideas from them, be it a restaurant.com voucher, a gorgeous vase you bought at a charity store, clothes you bought at a vintage store, or anything from Groupon Goods, a swap meet, eBay or Etsy. Or you can take them to the theater. Give them a "certificate" that you make for a night at a play or for somewhere else you're going to take them.

If it's the birthday of a guy or gal you are dating, it can be a "certificate" for a sexy night somewhere with *you*.

One Person's Junk is Another Person's Treasure

Then, of course, there's always regifting. If you received something at your birthday party that you didn't want or use, pass it on! This also works for things you may have had for some time, but never used. Just make sure they look new and in good condition. Then giftwrap the item and make it look special.

> "A friend never defends a husband who gets his wife an electric skillet for her birthday." –Erma Bombeck

Personally Yours

What's always wonderful is to get or make something "personal" for your friends' or family's special occasions. Whether it's writing a poem about them and framing it, or making a collage or a short film, nothing says you care more than something personal. If it's something sweet, that's perfect. If it's something funny, that's better!

Personal gifts mean thinking of that specific person when you give a gift. It doesn't have to be expensive. In fact, it doesn't have to cost anything at all. It just has to be meaningful to the recipient.

Call Me Martin Scorsese!

For my former boyfriend, I always made personal gifts. Dennis was an avid bicyclist and was going to do a major mountain biking trip through woods and mountains. Keep in mind, he was bald and wore glasses.

The movie *The Blair Witch Project* had recently come out and was a big hit. So I made him a 10-minute short film, *The No Hair Witch Project*. I grabbed a few friends to help me film it. When he wasn't around, I borrowed his bicycle, dressed in his bicycle clothes and helmet, and had my friends film me riding.

I wore a pair of glasses like his, and then when I took the helmet off – I had even put a bald pate over my hair! When he first saw the movie, he thought it was him!

He couldn't believe it. There were other fun parts in the movie, too – like when I pretended he had gotten lost in the woods, and I wore a flannel shirt and put a big belly under it, like Ned Beatty's character in *Deliverance*. I won't say what I was pretending to "do" to him, but if you've seen the movie, you can imagine it made a verrrrry funny parody of a memorable scene from it.

There were many things in that short little movie that were meaningful for me and Dennis, and we had tons of laughs watching it over and over. He loved that more than any other present he'd ever received from anyone!

And my friends who helped me make it had loads of fun that day, too. I even filmed each of *them* riding a bike with a bald pate and glasses, looking just like Dennis. It was a special birthday for all of us.

I've also made funny short films for my parents' birthdays and anniversaries, as well as writing poems and creating collages.

The point is these presents were always received with more joy than if I had bought an expensive gift of jewelry, art or clothing. Something personal always makes a splash – and if you're at a party with other people when you present it, it always gets "oohs and aahs."

When I made a funny collage for a girlfriend's wedding shower, another guest loved it so much, she offered to buy one from me so she could give it to another bride-to-be whose shower was coming up in a few weeks.

> "I'm not materialistic. I believe in presents from the heart, like a drawing that a child does." –Victoria Beckham

Regifting Tidbit

I was going to a party for a single girlfriend of mine, and didn't have a clue about what to give her.

About a week before her big day, I was at a nightclub and met a handsome guy from Argentina. He had a Brazilian accent, which made him sound ever so suave and dashing. He was interested in me, but sadly, I never seem to go for guys with accents (I don't think they "get" my humor). So I rarely date them.

However, my girlfriend Cindy LOVES guys with accents. Well, this was a perfectly timed coincidence. When he asked for my number, I told him I wasn't available, but I had a girlfriend who I thought he would hit it off with. I indicated her birthday was the following week, and asked him if I could "give him to her" for her birthday.

He was game. At Cindy's party, I presented her with a "gift certificate" for a date with Eduardo! All the guests laughed, and Cindy truly appreciated it.

When Eduardo took her out a week later, not only did he take her to dinner and dancing – he brought her flowers. And at the end of the date, he invited her to go to Hawaii with him! And I had given this man away to *her* instead of keeping him for myself! (They dated a few more times but, as it turned out, she didn't go with him to Hawaii. She was still hung-up on her ex, so we both stupidly let this great guy get away.)

"One woman's frog is another woman's prince" – Marilyn Anderson, *Never Kiss a Frog: A Girl's Guide to Creatures from the Dating Swamp.*

Celebrate and Sale-a-vate!

HOLIDAYS GALORE – Fourth of July, Memorial Day, Labor Day, Christmas, New Years, You Name it Day!

Many restaurants and businesses offer specials for various holidays. Sometimes, whole shopping areas close off streets to have a fair or celebration outdoors.

"Once again, we come to the Holiday Season, a deeply religious time that each of us observes, in his own way, by going to the mall of his choice." –Dave Barry

All the different holidays offer sales opportunities. Christmas, New Years, President's Day, Memorial Day, Labor Day and many other holidays usually mean big savings and special events, too. Also, if you travel, remember that other countries have different holidays, so consider where you will be and check to see if there's a holiday that might mean extra savings or fun for you.

My friend John likes the U.K. because they celebrate his birthday as a national holiday: Guy Fawkes Day. France has Bastille Day. Germany has Oktoberfest, which lasts a whole month. Brazil has its Day of the Dead, which is an amazingly fun festival for the living!

Holy days, much like holidays, are celebrated year-round. Depending on the religion, you may find retailers offering specials to draw you in.

> "Let's spend Thanksgiving spilling food on our clothes,
> and Black Friday buying new ones." –Unknown

Black Friday offers huge sales based on the religious holy days. It seems to start earlier each year and extends to Cyber Monday. Some of the best prices of the year can be found then.

> "I love giving gifts and I love receiving them. I really like giving little kids extravagant gifts. You see their little faces light up and they get excited. If it's a really good gift, I love receiving it, like jewels, small islands."
> –Gina Gershon

These day-after-Thanksgiving sales are colossal and the day-after-Christmas sales are sometimes even bigger! This is a terrific time to visit high-end department stores like Saks Fifth Avenue, Barneys or Neiman Marcus, which have blowout discounts in all their departments. Just know you'll be there with herds of other women trying to score designer fashions for bargainista prices.

Party Like a Mock Star!

In addition to the sales, holidays mean free events, concerts, blowouts and par-taaays! Only in this case, you don't have to be a star or a rock star to enjoy the happenings.

You can go with a friend or a whole group to revel in these – and it doesn't matter if you're rich or poor, a pauper or a millionaire!

For the **Fourth of July,** there are always lots of free concerts and free fireworks in almost all big cities.

These as well as other holiday celebrations are both fun and FREE to the public. On Memorial Day and July Fourth, many parks, beaches and communities feature concerts and picnics.

On Thanksgiving, some restaurants feature free festive meals for their regular patrons.

> **"Thanksgiving, man. Not a good day to be my pants."**
> **–Kevin James**

In Los Angeles, there are several restaurants that offer free dinners on Turkey Day, including **Café Gratitude** and **The Laff Factory**, which even includes a comedy show.

During the **Christmas holidays,** in areas with marinas, they often have holiday boat parades with wonderful lighting displays and fireworks. Sure, the rich folks with condos or houses by the water can watch from their windows . . . but *you don't have to live there* to enjoy the fun and views. Everyone can go to the beach or docksides to watch the festivities and have a ball.

Lots of neighborhoods have cool street fairs or block parties before Christmas. The stores are open for business and have special sales, along with free refreshments and music, even live carolers. Food might include appetizers, sandwiches, and desserts along with holiday beverages like eggnog, hot cocoa, mulled apple cider, wine, and champagne. It's fun to walk in and out of the shops even if you're not buying anything.

> **"Nothing says holidays like a cheese log." –Ellen Degeneres**

A few of my favorite streets for this are Main Street in Santa Monica and Abbott Kinney Boulevard in Venice. The shops on Montana

Avenue in Santa Monica do a similar night, as do some of the shops along Melrose Avenue in West Hollywood.

Check the local neighborhoods in your city during the holidays to see where there's a shopping area featuring one of these nights to stroll and schmooze through the stores.

In addition to shopping nights, many hotels or stores have tree-lighting ceremonies that are open to the public. These frequently have refreshments, music, and holiday cheer for those who attend.

Another major way for you to enjoy the holiday season is to give to others. Many organizations have parties that are open to the public if you bring a gift for Toys for Tots or other charitable organizations. This way you can enjoy a wonderful event and at the same time help others not as fortunate.

"That's the true spirit of Christmas; people being helped by people other than me." –Jerry Seinfeld

Businesses and companies usually have holiday parties as well, sometimes open to those who might have a need for their services in the future. Here, you can make new friends and potential business contacts, too.

If you go to **www.eventbrite.com** in your city, you will find all kinds of free parties and events, some of which ask you to bring an unwrapped toy for children.

Check on those that are in your area of interest or expertise, whether it's film and TV, the tech biz, women's events, financial organizations, etc.

I signed up for four of these events for this past year and posted them on my Facebook page so some of my friends could join me there.

Of course, there are also many opportunities to give during the holidays by volunteering to help serve food to the homeless, wrap gifts, or do other service-oriented tasks that can bring you happiness and new friends while you help others.

Meetups also often have holiday parties, and if you don't have family nearby to share happy times with, check out the so-called "orphan" meetups in your city. There's no reason to stay home alone or be by yourself. I've gone numerous times as a total stranger to a meetup Thanksgiving or Christmas dinner for "orphan adults" and they were always sociable and convivial evenings. Sometimes I even came away with a new close friend.

If you're shy, push through it; sometimes stepping out of your comfort zone can create new experiences and more joy in your life. Check out the different possibilities in your area at:

www.meetup.com

Christmas Eve always tends to be a quiet night. If you don't have friends to visit, or don't celebrate it, you can find other things to do. I think it's an unwritten rule from the Torah that on Christmas Day, if you're Jewish, you have to go for a movie and Chinese food!

Another super cool event, which I mentioned in the "That's Entertainment" chapter, is one I discovered on a trip during the holidays a few years ago. In Santa Fe, New Mexico, Christmas Eve is celebrated by the world-class art galleries on Canyon Road. They are all open, offering food, wine, and music to folks who stroll the paths (often snow-covered) going from gallery to gallery. Lanterns dot the walkway, with carolers singing and bonfires blazing where you can warm your hands. It's beautiful, fun, and free.

What Are You Doing New Year's Eve?

Then, there's the biggest holiday of all – **New Year's Eve!** That's when so many restaurants up their prices and charge exorbitant amounts for so-called special menus. But who says you have to go out to a restaurant and spend a small fortune? Not me!

Instead, on New Year's, there are all kinds of free concerts and fireworks in different areas of each city. I've been to popular events both in Marina del Rey, CA, and in Fort Lauderdale, Florida. And don't forget the fabulous Times Square in New York for sharing the excitement of the night. It's excellent free entertainment, and it doesn't matter if you're broke or if you have a load of cash in the bank.

There's always fun to be had without putting a dent in your wallet. (Just make sure you *hold onto* your wallet. When there are big crowds, you want to keep your handbags and wallets zippered tight and hold them close where they don't become a target for some sleazy, slippery pickpocket.)

So either eat at home, or pick an eatery that offers their regular menu, then head out for the fireworks, fun, and dancing in the street.

Before the Parade Passes By

Excellent for free entertainment on holidays are the parades in many cities, where you can bring the whole family.

Some of the more famous ones include **The Mummers Parade**, a New Year's Day tradition in Philadelphia, Pennsylvania; **Seminole Hard Rock Winterfest Boat Parade** in Fort Lauderdale, Florida;

The Rose Parade in Pasadena, California; **Macy's Thanksgiving Day Parade** in New York City; **Fourth of July Midnight Parade in** Gatlinburg, Tennessee; **St. Patrick's Day Parade** in Boston, **Mardi Gras** in New Orleans; **The Saint Paul Winter Carnival** in Saint Paul, Minnesota; and the **Chinese New Year Parade** in San Francisco.

Parades are great entertainment, and what's sometimes even more fun, is going to the site the next morning.

In Pasadena, *the day after* the Rose Parade, go check out all the floats. It's not as crowded and is definitely more leisurely than the parade itself, yet it still provides the "oohs and aahs" from seeing the floats and being much more "up close and personal" in order to see how the fabulous floats are made.

In NYC, the night before the Thanksgiving Parade is a huge deal, with people viewing the balloons on the ground, up close.

And don't forget Mardi Gras in New Orleans, where you can not only hear great music and see great floats, but also get free beads and see free boobs!

Not for shy, brooding types. Unless you want to let loose and join the jaunty flashers and the crowd repeatedly yelling, "Show us your tits!"

To find out about free events during the holidays and all year round, check your local papers or go online to sites like **www.Timeout.com** and **www.Eventful.com**; or else, you can just Google "events" or "free events" in your city.

Seasonal Savings

As the seasons change, you can take advantage of all kinds of special sales. Summer Savings, Back to School Specials, Winter White Sales, Spring into New Savings – all are examples of deals based on the change of seasons. Clothing is one of the things which have both seasons and "model years" that may offer you double savings. Toys also have both possible deals.

New Model Years

There are also manufacturers' "model year" sales. Each year, when a new model comes out for cars, electronics, fashions, etc., the "old" models go on sale. Ask a salesperson at the store; they should know when their items change model years. If you don't need the absolute latest model, you can still get something that's brand new . . . and save big time!

Sports Celebrations

During the year, each sport has playoffs and championships offering excuses to celebrate. Retailers take advantage of these to get customers to buy their wares.

Whether it's basketball, baseball, soccer, hockey, or the biggest one, the Super Bowl, there are many deals to be had when these are celebrated. An example is that stores like Best Buy and Target offer super deals on big-screen TVs right before Super Bowl Sunday. Play it right, and you can make it your super sale day, too! And don't forget to check out pre-game tickets that can be inexpensive as well.

And the Award Goes To . . .

You don't have to win . . . you don't have to be nominated . . . you don't even have to be in the biz. You just have to party!

In Hollywood, New York and Nashville, there are all kinds of celebrations for award shows. Whether it's the Oscars, Emmys, Grammys, American Music Awards or the myriad of different awards offered each year, there are always parties and events going on.

I mention in the *That's Entertainment* chapter that you can even get to go to the award shows as a "seat filler." When a celebrity needs to get up, the producers need to fill the seat in the audience. You can rent a gown and jewelry for the night and become a "star" like Cinderella. (I might not do the glass slipper thing, though, because I'm a klutz; I'd fall, the shoe would break, I'd get slivers of glass in my feet and end up at the podiatrist!)

> "Cameron Diaz was so cute at the MTV Movie Awards when she pulled her skirt up and wiped her armpits."
> –Pink

Chap Wrap 'n Recap

- Birthday Parties
- Birthday Freebies
- Gifties and Goodies
- Making It Personal
- Holidays and Hollywood Happenings

Birthday Quiz: True or False?

On your birthday:

1. It's best to stay home and bury your head under the covers and be depressed you're getting older.
2. You can fly in a kite over the Pacific Ocean for free.
3. Go down to the soup kitchen for a meal with the rest of your unemployed friends.
4. Add one more line to your suicide note.
5. Go to your local hospital and sell a pint of blood so you'll get a donut and maybe have enough money for a burrito at Taco Bell.
6. Inviting 40 people to a party means you're not gonna be able to pay your bills the next six months.
7. Don't tell anyone it's your birthday, because no one cares, and they all hate you, 'cause you're a cheap bastard.

11. The Whole Enchilada and Other Assorted Tidbits

What's the Whole Enchilada? Getting it *all* for free. How can you live like a millionaire when you're a million short – in all the categories all the time?

Write it. Live it.

There are people who live the elite life by writing about it. Maybe not *all* the time, but much of the time. Some travel writers are lucky enough to go around the world, staying at exclusive places, dining at fine restaurants and seeing all that various countries have to offer . . . because they are writing about it in top magazines. In "Getaways and Globetrotting Galore," I tell how I accidentally started travel reporting and getting many of the perks that go with it. It was only a part-time thing for me, so I didn't go whole hog (or whole millionaire) – but when I did, I always had a grand time. There are some travel reporters who do it full time and year 'round. They are constantly on the road, delivering stories and meeting deadlines – but they are able to travel the world and enjoy the benefits.

> "It's easier to find a traveling companion than to get rid of one." –Art Buchwald

However, special events and ultra-hip happenings *in your own city* are there for the taking! When you're a magazine or newspaper reporter, or even a blogger with a good following, you can get on guest lists to attend all kinds of celebrity parties, red carpet events, and posh affairs. After you start a column, contact publicists in your area, write about their clients, and become friends with them. You'll get invites to keep you busy all year long.

Whenever I wrote about events or took trips, I always had the best times. On the road, whenever I stayed at hotels, upon arrival I'd always receive welcome baskets with wine, cheese, snacks and a card thanking me for being there! And I didn't just write about hotels and restaurants. I once wrote about designer eyeglasses – and the company sent me eight pairs! I had a friend who wrote about designer clothes . . . and she was sent fabulous clothes all the time. Another blogger acquaintance wrote about handbags – and got handbags to die for! My friend who wrote a column about cars – got a new car to drive every two weeks for many years! So obviously, one way to get "the whole enchilada" is to be a writer – and make it your living or a fun-filled hobby that can get you living like a millionaire.

> "I've been to almost as many places as my luggage." — Bob Hope

Is It Smarter to Barter?

Another way that some people get everything in life for free is to barter. I've never done this per se, although I have written articles in exchange for goods or services. No matter what kind of items you might want to swap, there are many websites that list an abundance of bartering opportunities. You can sign up with something you're willing to offer, and get all kinds of things in exchange for them. People barter services as well as goods. Trade legal help for accounting services. Trade massage therapy for mental therapy. You can exchange cars and even houses. I've never used bartering sites, so I'd recommend you check out other experts or sites about this. But it can be done; in fact, there are folks who almost never use money to buy anything. Some bartering sites offer a variety of things for trading; others are specific for particular kinds of goods or services.

www.u-exchange.com

www.BarterOnly.com

www.tradeaway.com

www.Listia.com

www.freecycle.org

www.freegan.info

www.BizX.com

www.SwapaCD.com

www.SwapaDVD.com

The point is, if you go online, you can probably find a place to swap anything you have or want.

Money You Don't Even Know You Have!

Speaking of going online, there are a few sites you'll definitely want to visit – and soon! Believe it or not, there are gazillions of dollars just sitting and waiting for people to simply claim what they are owed. **www.unclaimed.org** is the National Association of Unclaimed Property Administrators (Naupa).

Wait a minute, you say. *"I don't have unclaimed property."* The truth is most people don't realize they have it. In 2015 alone, $3,235 billion was returned to its rightful owners out of $7,763 billion collected! The money is from abandoned or forgotten accounts in financial institutions with no activity for a year or longer. It could be from old savings or checking accounts, stocks, uncashed dividends, insurance policies, security deposits, IRS refunds and more. It could be *your* money sitting in unclaimed property or possibly that of your parents, grandparents or great-grandparents. Plus, over the years, it may have accrued some healthy interest.

Individual states maintain the funds, so you should check all the places where you or your family lived at any time. **www.MissingMoney.com** will assist you in thoroughly searching all participating states to find your family's missing, lost, and unclaimed property, money and assets.

I told a friend I saw his name on the list, and he didn't believe me. I literally had to force him to file for money that was rightfully his. Even when a state where he lived 20 years before sent him a notice saying they were sending him a payment, he refused to believe it and thought it was a scam. It wasn't. It took almost a year, but he eventually received a check for $8,000! Okay, it wasn't a million, but it was still "found" money. So, make sure you check the sites and see if you have a stash of cash you didn't know existed. It's free to look or to make a claim, so what are you waiting for?

Find Your Crowd to Fund Your Fun

One somewhat contemporary way to get large sums of money for the important things in your life is to do crowdfunding. In recent years, crowdfunding has become immensely popular with people who want to raise money for artistic projects like movies, books, inventions, and entrepreneurial endeavors. It's also been used to fundraise for medical bills, surgery, funerals, and even a wedding. These days, people can ask for money for anything! And it's not unusual for someone out there in the webosphere . . . to give it to them.

Oftentimes, to start, you'll be asking friends and family. But depending on the specific campaign, sometimes strangers become a part of it and they help you in your pursuit of a dream or a miracle – and give you dough. There are crowdfunding sites where people raise money to travel, and some have even crowdfunded trips around the world. Niche sites catering to particular interests abound. I just discovered a bizarre and bodacious site where strangers can "invest in breasts." It's called www.MyFreeImplants.com. Cool, huh? A way for broke bimbos to get big boobies from big-hearted boobs!

Check these other, not-quite-so-specialized crowdfunding sites to see the wealth of things people are raising money for, and that you could, too. Please note, there are differences between platforms regarding the types of projects and backers, and the level of support and fees.

www.Kickstarter.com

www.Indiegogo.com

www.GoFundMe.com

www.Fundable.com

www.YouCaring.com

www.RocketHub.com

www.PubLaunch.com

www.FundAnything.com

Of course, the thing to realize about crowdfunding is that not everyone reaches their monetary goal. For every super-successful campaign – and there have been some that made many thousands of dollars – there are hundreds of other campaigns that failed. It's also not without work and effort. The truly successful campaigns are those from people or projects that are not only worthy, but that spend hours, days, weeks, and months in preparation and planning in order to achieve their goal.

Assorted Sites for Bargain Tips and Saving Snippets

By now, you've realized there is a never-ending world of information on how to get things and do things in a less expensive, cheaper, more economical, practical, and fun way. I can't list them all; different sites may come and go; various opportunities can present themselves at different times. I've tried to open your eyes and your wallet to the possibilities. You can use those I've mentioned or search for more on your own. Here are a few websites, not previously mentioned, for interesting money-saving info:

www.moneycrashers.com

www.wisebread.com

www.lenpenzo.com

www.moneytalksnews.com

www.bradsdeals.com

www.thepennyhoarder.com

www.slickdeals.com

www.shoplocal.com

www.livingwellspendingless.com

www.swagbucks.com

Save Money and/or Make Money, Too

If you're creative, you can not only find ways to *save* money – you can find ways to *make* money. These sites offer opportunities to become a buyer or a seller. It's a win-win for both.

www.elance.com

www.taskrabbit.com

www.freelance.com

www.freelancer.com

www.99designs.com

www.guru.com

www.upwork.com

www.ifreelance.com

www.peopleperhour.com

www.handy.com

www.fiverr.com

www.tongal.com

www.cafepress.com

www.zazzle.com

A Penny for Your Thoughts . . . or High Priced Items?

Do you love the excitement of gambling? If you don't mind putting money up for a product and possibly . . . er, *probably* not winning it, then penny auctions might be for you. I've never tried them, but they advertise up to as much as *99 percent off* for all kinds of expensive electronics and other costly items. You can get an iPad for $12 or a HD TV for $29. On Beezid in 2010, a lucky guy won the bid and got a new Ford Mustang for $719. In May of 2016, someone got a Jeep Wrangler for 99 cents! I don't know how much it cost him to win, but you can bet a ton of other bidders spent a of bunch of bucks trying.

Apparently, it takes both dedication and strategy to bid in penny auctions, and there are many, such as **www.HappyBidDay.com**, **www.Quibids.com**, **www.OrangeBidz.com**, **www.Beezid.com**, and **www.DealDash.com**. I find these sites overwhelming, and I don't have the stomach or personality to participate in them. However, if you want to know more about how they work, try checking out several sites that review them and give the details on each:

www.BestPennyAuctionSites.Org

www.PennyAuctionPolice.com

www.PennyAuctionWatch.com

Another different kind of auction site from the CEO of Quibids is **www.TumbleDeal.com** – a *price drop deal* site, where the cost of an item goes *down* until someone buys it. What about a site where things cost zero? Oh, wait a minute, they exist! As I've mentioned before, you can get things absolutely free on Craigslist, as well as on recycling or bartering sites. But the items won't be new, like they are on the Auction Penny Sites where you probably won't win the item anyway.

An Appetite for Apps

In addition to the web, there are all kinds of money-saving apps available on your smartphone. I don't use many apps, and my smartphone acts more like a dumbphone, but these articles list a slew of popular apps for budgeting and saving bucks.

> www.lifehack.org/articles/money/25-apps-that-will-save-you-lots-money.html
>
> www.ourfreakingbudget.com/best-budgeting-saving-apps-of-2016/
>
> www.gottabemobile.com/2016/06/09/best-budget-apps/
>
> www.allyou.com/smartshopping/saving-money
>
> www.nylon.com/articles/money-saving-apps-2015

"What's the use of happiness? It can't buy you money."
—Henny Youngman

Chap Wrap 'n Recap

- Travel Writing
- Bartering
- Crowdfunding
- Web Surfing for Savings
- Online Bidding for Bargains
- Apps

The Whole Enchilada Quiz

Fill in the blanks with the correct answers:

a) free b) $20,000 c) 99 cents d) zero e) boobies

1. A lucky guy bought a jeep on a Penny Auction site for
   _____.
2. If you're a travel writer, you can see the world for
   practically _____.
3. If you're diligent, you can furnish your whole house from
   Craigslist for _____.
4. Crowdfunding has raised money for things like movies,
   books, funerals and _____.
5. You could find $20 you lost in a drawer, or _____ that's
   yours in unclaimed property.

Answers:

1. c.
2. d.
3. a. or d.
4. e.
5. b.

12. Rules to Live (Like a Millionaire) By

"It's a way of looking at the world . . . and seeing infinite possibilities." –Marilyn Anderson

Everyone has heard the phrase "Rules to Live By." Many different writers or speakers discuss them, and they usually describe ways to keep a positive attitude and a happy life. I certainly agree with that, but I also have my own set of rules. They are simple and I call them:

Rules to Live (Like a Millionaire) By:

1. Ask

2. Negotiate

3. Make friends

4. Be open

5. Know the things you want

6. Carpe diem

7. Be creative

8. Have fun along the way

9. Don't worry about the things you can't control

1. ASK – Make an "Ask" of Yourself.

This Number One rule is about the simplest, and it's amazing to me that more people don't do it. By simply "asking" at various times, you can save a boatload of money. I've done it and saved hundreds, even thousands. I'll give you some examples, starting with a little one.

Years ago I had this pretty white throw rug. I loved it, but as you can imagine, white can get extremely dirty, extremely fast. When the white had turned to grey (not quite), it was time to get it cleaned. I called the best local rug cleaners in my neighborhood, and asked how much it would cost to get it cleaned, and they told me $80. That was a lot for me at the time. So instead of just saying, "Okay," or "Thanks for your time," I *asked*: "Are you having any sales coming up?" Without hesitation, the girl on the phone answered. "Well, you know, we do have a 2-for-1 special." Notice she said, "Well, you know!" No, I didn't know. But by making an "ask" of myself, I now did. I thanked her and hung up. Of course the problem was, I didn't have two rugs, I had one rug. But I had a lot of girlfriends. So they each got a call from me, asking: "Do you have a rug that needs cleaning?" Well, guess what – one of my friends had a dirty rug, too – so instead of each paying $80, we each paid $40, because I simply asked, "Do you have any sales coming up?"

Another time I was in a department store and saw a fabulous royal blue cashmere jacket for $1000. I loved it but couldn't afford it. I "asked" if it would be going on sale. Then I *asked* the salesgirl if she could call me when it went on sale. I tell the whole amazing story in the "So You Think You Can Shop" Chapter, but suffice it to say, I got that luscious cashmere jacket for $149!

When you're shopping for computers or electronics, it's also a great time to make an "ask" of yourself. Computers are expensive. If you find one you like and it's too pricey, ask if there are any specials or "open box" items. When buying a car, ask when their new models are expected; all the prices of the current year will be reduced then. Also, whenever you're about to make a big purchase, it's good to *ask* around. Ask your friends where they find their bargains, or if they know of any deals.

Once, I even got an $8,000 trip totally FREE because I made an "ask" of myself. I tell that story in the "Giving, Getting, and Galavanting" Chapter.

There's another truly fun experience I had making an "ask" of myself, even though it doesn't pertain to shopping. It pertains to men. Okay, I was man-shopping! I was taking a trip to Puerto Rico, and this was in the years when planes had smoking and non-smoking sections, and seat assignments were given at the check-in counter. After I said "no-smoking," the reservations clerk asked me where I preferred to sit, "Aisle or window seat?" I asked her, "Can you just put me next to a handsome man?" She laughed, then replied, "Why don't you just stand over to the side, and when you see someone you like, give me a signal." "Oh no," I said, embarrassed and blushing, "That's okay, I was just kidding."

A half hour later I am on the plane, sitting in an aisle seat. A gorgeous guy comes walking down the aisle and stops in front of me. He points toward the window, "Looks like that's my seat." He puts his bags in the overhead compartment, and takes the window seat next to mine. Glancing at me, he smiles. I smile back. Then he says, "Something really funny happened when I checked in." "Oh?" I replied." "Yeah, as soon as I told the desk clerk I wanted 'no-smoking,' she said, 'Have I got the seat for you!'"

The best part of the story was that he and I talked through the entire flight, and when we arrived in Puerto Rico, he invited me out for dinner that night. We ended up spending most of the week together. And of course, he paid for everything. I had a blast on my vacation – all because I "asked" when I checked in at the counter.

The bottom line is, if you make an "ask" of yourself, you can save all kinds of money and still enjoy the best for less. And maybe even meet a sweetie!

2. Negotiate – "Let's Make a Deal"

There are certain times when people are used to negotiating. One is in business deals. Another time is when you're buying a car. What most folks don't realize is that you can negotiate in lots of places other than auto dealerships. Aha, you say! You remember a time when you were on vacation in a foreign country, and the travel book told you to haggle with the street vendors. They expect it. Yes, that's where it works.

But even in the U.S., even in major stores, the fact is you can often negotiate there, too. For instance, many different kinds of stores will *match prices*. This includes chain stores selling electronics, as well as some department stores.

Staples may advertise they have products "on sale," but frequently their sale prices are still *above the prices* at which other stores are selling the items. At both Staples and Best Buy, they will match prices with other retail stores – and also with Amazon.com. So don't just accept the price they are charging for a product. No. Do your research . . . by looking online, finding the best price for the exact same item, and telling the sales clerk. Then, negotiate to get the best deal. There are even apps to find products by their skew number, so you can use your phone and find the best price right there.

The same is true of Nordstrom; they will match prices if another store is selling the same item for less. Believe it or not, I've even "negotiated" with the salesgirl at Nordstrom. See my story in "So You Think You Can Shop." I still have that beautiful blue cashmere blazer. No matter what kind of store you are in, you can always try to negotiate, and you can ask if they match prices. With the Internet, it's so easy to check on prices and find the best one. Still, you may want to go to your favorite store where you can try it on or see it in person. But doing your research and negotiating can save you both money and time.

As far as cars go, negotiating can be intense, but you have to do it. It's expected. Of course, not everyone is a good negotiator, so if you are not one, find someone who is and take them along. My friend, Stan, loves to help people find car deals. He has bought more than fifty cars and knows the way it works. Stan boasts that he saves hundreds, if not thousands, on each deal. One trick is to always say that you don't have a trade-in and negotiate the deal without it. Once you've done that, you can change your mind and tell them you *do* have a trade-in! This way, you'll know what they are really giving you for your car. Frankly, I don't believe in trading a car in, since you will always get a better deal selling it yourself. However, if you don't want to go through the hassle of advertising it or having strangers coming to see it, I recommend going to a used car lot. You will still get a better deal than a trade-in. I've sold my last two cars that way . . . and still negotiated. I had two different used car dealers across the street from each other bidding against each other for my old Honda Prelude!

Another tip about car dealers. When it is the last day of a promotion or a month, the salespersons are more motivated to make the deal happen, because they get spiffs. Spiffs are extra bonuses for hitting a certain level of sales. So when the salesperson is under pressure and extremely self-motivated, they will do what it takes to make the deal happen. Remember: the answer is always "no," unless you "ask". **So ask for the deal you want, no matter how crazy it sounds.** There is always another place that will give you a deal, and they know it. So keep that in mind: Negotiate, do your research, and say, "Let's make a deal!" There are also numerous sites to help when you're buying either new or used. If you don't want to negotiate, there are car buying services at CarMax, Costco and AAA. Check out CarPriceSecrets.com and TrueCar.com as well.

3. Make Friends – "You Got to Have *SALES* Friends!"

This makes sense in so many ways. I always make friends with the shop people so that they get to know me and tell me when something I want goes on sale. When I tried on a designer dress that I loved but couldn't afford, my new salesgirl friend took my number and called me a few weeks later: "That Marc Jacobs dress you loved just went on sale!" It's also smart to make friends at computer and electronics stores. I was buying a new laptop at Microsoft and it was above my budget. But I made friends with the sales associate, and he found a way to give me the "student" discount, which was about $300 less than the regular price. (I told him I was a student of life, and of the anatomy of the human male.)

I try to develop a relationship with salespeople wherever I shop, especially for high priced items. Then I bring my friends and family to them personally, so when I return to buy something, I remind them of all the business that I brought them. They give deals to my friends, and I get the super deal!

So think of all those songs with "friend" in the title, and then add the word "sales" in front of it...

"With a Little Help from My SALES Friend!" (The Beatles)

"You've Got a SALES Friend" (Carole King)

"That's What SALES Friends are For!" (Dionne Warwick)

"You've got a SALES Friend in Me!" (Randy Newman)

It's worth building these relationships; they literally pay off!

Of course, the other part of "making friends" is to make friends with wealthy people. One of my guy friends was broke all the time. But he was a comic, and women found him charming and funny. They loved having him around. More than that, they were physically attracted to him and, since they were well-off, it didn't matter to them that he didn't have a pot to piss in! He dated some famous celebrities who'd take him to all kinds of expensive events and galas. He even got several marriage proposals from rich women, but declined. One dazzling diva invited him to move into her luxurious mansion on one condition: he wasn't allowed to leave his beat-up car in front of her house, so he always had to park at the bottom of the hillside and walk up the cliff.

Another gal I know made good friends with her elderly neighbor across the hall. Taryn was a singer who didn't make much money, but she had a good heart. She would help the man with his shopping and take him to his doctor appointments all the time. He had been a school teacher and loved literature, but his eyesight had gone bad, so she read books to him two nights a week. When he passed away, she got a big surprise. He had a huge bank account and left a significant amount to her.

In both situations, the less affluent people were being their authentic selves. They went into the friendships naturally and for good reasons. Perhaps it can work for you as well. Mixing and mingling with people wealthier than you can be illuminating and gratifying. You may learn new things and possibly even ways to attract money yourself. Think of what you have to offer to others, and give graciously without expectations. If you create good karma, it may come back to you. In any case, you can't go wrong being a good friend to someone.

4. Be Open – Try. Something. New.

So many wonderful things in my life have come to me unplanned and unexpectedly. These included one-time-only situations as well as experiences that changed the course of my life in a positive way. Ultimately, what made them possible is the fact I was open to them. They might have been new and unfamiliar, or even somewhat out of my comfort zone, but because I was open to different things, I went with them and ended up having all kinds of rewarding experiences. I was auctioned off as a bachelorette auction for charity (see the chapter "Giving, Getting, and Gala-vanting"); I did hot laps at a race car course (See "Getaways and Globetrotting Galore"); I started a travel column and went all across the country and on a five-star vacation to Taiwan (see "Getaways and Globetrotting Galore"); I've had a comped dinner with millionaires at a Wolfgang Puck restaurant (see "Eats, Treats, and Feats"); I've been to opening night at the Ahmanson Theatre and to the closing night at an art gallery (see

"That's Entertainment"). Sometimes, I got the offer in advance, and had a while to decide on it; other times I had to make a split-second decision. The fact is, I was open to the possibilities, and they provided me great joy. *You can do the same if you are open to new things.*

When you are open to new possibilities, amazing things can happen; in fact, frequently, the best things happen when they are not planned. Other people sense your ease when you are able to roll with life, and you'll be the person they call for something special if they know you are open and flexible. So next time someone invites you somewhere new, say yes! Or instead of staying home one night, go out. Or if there's something you've wanted to try that you haven't, do it! You only go around once, so start saying "yes" to the many new things that await you.

5. Know the Things You Want

If you could have anything you wanted, what would it be? A new car? A diamond bracelet? A trip to Italy? Tahiti? Africa?

Many a time, people don't focus on what makes them happy. They are too busy doing "life." So take time to think about what you wish to experience that can spark happiness in you. If it's a dream, let go of anything that says "It's impossible." If it's a bucket list, know you can accomplish it.

Some folks are into visualizing. They say if you "visualize" something, you can make it come true. For instance, visualize yourself in Tahiti, and one day you may be there. This certainly can't hurt, and it can be fun. Closing your eyes and picturing yourself on a serene tropical beach, sipping a coconut matai with a handsome, bronzed-tanned man fanning you – what can be bad about that? You can certainly enjoy the moment when you are visualizing it. It can give you pleasure, contentment, joy. Sounds good to me.

Others believe you can chant for what you want. If the truth be told, years ago, I did some chanting. Not the usual kind. I didn't sit alone by myself, in a spiritual setting and chant, over and over, for what I wanted. (I'm far too Type A to sit and meditatively chant.) But I figured, "Hey, chanting can't hurt!" So, as I was driving to my job for a TV show where I worked as a temp secretary, I would "chant" on the way to work. Yep, I would be behind the wheel, as I rolled down Santa Monica Boulevard toward Paramount Pictures at nine in the morning, chanting, *"Nam myoho renge kyo."* I was chanting for a writing assignment. Did it work? Well, I'm not sure if was the chanting, but somewhere in the middle of the season, the boss called me into his office. I pitched several stories, and he actually gave me a writing assignment. My very first TV writing job! Was it the chanting? Who knows? The point is, I knew what I wanted, and I was prepared. I was in the right place at the right time. And I was ready.

But my point here isn't about chanting or visualizing – it's about knowing what you want and being prepared for the possibilities that may arise toward achieving it.

Make a list of the things that would make you happy. Write them down, visualize, chant, put yourself in the right environment – whatever feels comfortable for you. The point is – KNOW WHAT YOU WANT, and remember it, so that if an opportunity presents itself, you're ready to GO FOR IT.

Another example is my Canyon Ranch Spa story in the chapter on "Giving, Getting, and Gala-vanting." A wealthy girlfriend used to tell me about this fabulous spa she went to, and I remembered that if I ever had the chance – or the money – I would go there. Then, when I needed to get something donated to charity, I called Canyon Ranch . . . and they donated a trip for me and my date! I remembered something I wanted and, when the opportunity presented itself, I was ready. *Carpe diem!*

6. Carpe Diem

Seize the day! This is about being spontaneous to opportunities that suddenly "show up" for you. Lucky people are those who are ready when life offers possibilities. *Carpe diem* is an attitude of willingness to be spontaneous and to take action.

Fate favors the prepared. I've had times when I was invited on a trip at the last minute. Eeek, how to get ready, what to take? No problem. I always have a bag packed with two days of clothes and supplies so if someone invites me for a weekend getaway to the Bahamas or wherever, I am prepared. Those Girl Scout trainings have paid off! It might only be a day trip or a shopping excursion, but being flexible enough to take advantage of opportunities the moment they arrive makes life more adventurous and fun. Since I live in Los Angeles, it's also good to have this bag packed in case of an earthquake!

Another secret is to hide mad money in various places, so if you need to make a special purchase, you can dip into it and be able to take advantage of a great deal at the last minute. Stow some away in a nook or cranny of your car, too. If you lose your wallet or it gets stolen, it's always good to have a secret stash of cash.

Seizing the day is also about making each day count. Life is precious, and we never know what's going to happen. So, doesn't it make sense to enjoy the moment now? Have flexibility when needed. But most of all, try to have fun.

7. Be Creative

Creativity is available to all of us. Even if you think you are not particularly creative, let that thought go and imagine you are. Ask yourself, "What would a creative person do here?"

Necessity is the mother of invention. You might not have a lot of money, but you can be resourceful and create some wonderful experiences. For example, when I wanted to impress a new guy I was dating, I decorated my place like an Italian Bistro and served "home-made" Fettuccine Alfredo. He was thrilled and loved it more than if we had gone to an expensive restaurant. (He never guessed I bought the pre-made pasta at Costco!)

I frequently make my own gifts for friends and family, and they always love the personal touch. I've made personal movies, cards, collages, CDs, even personal calendars . . . and my friends cherish them.

Speaking of Italian, I made a little movie for a boyfriend where I played an old Italian woman cooking, and I even pasted fake hair under my armpits! We had some hearty laughs watching it. As I lifted my hand to stir the pot, the fuzzy tufts under my arm fell off and floated to the floor.

Check out the Internet for DIY ideas. If you can imagine it, there is probably someone that posted a video, showing you how to do it. Just follow instructions and, presto – you can be a creative genius! It doesn't have to be professional; it just has to be personal, and it will be appreciated.

If it doesn't work one way, try another. I always dreamed of having a movie produced, and I worked years in show business to achieve that goal. One of my screenplays was optioned eight times by different

Hollywood producers, who never got it made. Finally, I decided "no more options." That's when things started to happen. I found an investor, and within six months my film was cast and in production. The movie is now out on Amazon, iTunes, and on DVD in Walmart stores. **www.HowtoBeataBullyTheMovie.com**

8. Have Fun Along the Way

The most important thing in life is to have fun. It's about enjoying your life, and not just slaving away and being like Scrooge. When the miserly codger finally decided he wanted to make people happy, he began enjoying his life!

I'm hoping the stories and tips in this book will contribute more fun to your life. And not just fun, but fun for less money!

It's also important to realize that things don't have to be "perfect." I know many authors who make themselves miserable trying to make their work absolutely perfect. Now, there's no question that rewriting is always necessary, but some people keep reworking it and reworking it for decades. The result is it never gets finished. I've learned sometimes "done" is better than perfect. As a writer, I know you can spend hours, days and months trying to fix a chapter, a paragraph, a sentence, or even a single word. You want to make your work its best before you show it to anyone. But if it doesn't go out into the world, it never gets seen. It's like a tree falling in a forest. If there's no one to hear it, there's no sound. So at some point, you have to say it's ready. There will always be changes you can make. Even Academy Award winners confess there are things in their films they wish they could fix. (So if you don't find this book perfect, please forgive me. I wanted it out in the world so you could read it and enjoy!)

If you wait around for something to be perfect, you may miss the experience altogether. The same is true for dating and romance. So many women I know have their idea of the perfect man. These gals have a list, and if a guy doesn't match up to every item on that list, he's out. I feel differently. I try to look for the good in every person – and every guy – even if he's not "the one."

For example, I realized almost immediately that a particular guy I met on a dating site wasn't a romantic match for me. But because we had a lot of common interests and were both open to being "friends," we ended up being business partners. We've had a ton of cool experiences, and have even made some money together. And had lots of fun along the way! (And it wasn't "friends with benefits," either. Although that works for some people, too!)

This is true for all aspects of your life. Try to find the good in every day, in every situation, and in every person that you meet. Choose to have fun. Relish the fact you can do many wonderful things in life, and in this book, without spending a fortune.

9. Don't Worry About the Things You Can't Control

So much in life happens without you having any input. I live in Los Angeles, which has earthquakes. Some people worry about the Big One. Not me. If it happens, it happens. I'd rather live here than where they have hurricanes. At least, if there's a quake, my hair won't get wet!

When I did experience an earthquake in 1994, FEMA paid me to move, and they paid my rent in the new place for six months. Not only that, but I met some great folks I wouldn't have otherwise. And I liked my new apartment better, too. I'm waiting for the next one . . . so I can get an apartment that's even better still.

When my first book, *Never Kiss a Frog: A Girl's Guide to Creatures from the Dating Swamp,* was soon to come out, the *Los Angeles Times* had a column about a dating coach who discussed turning men into frogs. My first thought was, "Oh no, I've been scooped. Now the *Times* will never write about my book."

Then I decided to turn lemons into lemonade. I wrote a letter to the editor responding to the column, and expressing my own philosophy on frogs. I signed it as the author of *Never Kiss a Frog.* The following week, *my letter* appeared in the newspaper! It was the first publicity I got for my book, which wasn't even out yet. Plus, the *Los Angeles Times* hired me to write several more articles.

What's the point of getting yourself in a frazzle if you can't do anything about it? If you're not a millionaire – and you might never be one – so what? Take pleasure in the things you *can* do, and the friends you have, and the good times in your life. And get out there and *Live Like a Millionaire When You're a Million Short.*

Chap Wrap 'n Recap

C'mon, guys, you want the wrap?
Just go back to the start of the chap!
It's all there, but I'll do it now in rap
And go over it in rhyme in order to recap.

Make an "ask" of yourself wherever you go
Don't be an "ass" or a big fat schmo.
Prices at stores are all in fluctuation
So do your research and try negotiation.

Make friends with sales clerks and rich folks, too
You'd be surprised how they might help you.
If you know what you want and don't forget it
A great opportunity may arise if you let it.

Be creative and open to new possibilities
You'll get invited to all kinds of festivities.
Remember *Carpe Diem* and Seize the Day
And please make sure to have fun along the way!

Don't worry if you can't control a situation
Go with the flow, and save your perspiration.
No matter if you're rich or poor, don't be lax
Life's meant to be enjoyed, so live it to the max!

Rules to Live (Like a Millionaire) By Quiz

What is more creative?

1. You invite a friend to Appleby's for lunch.
2. You invite a friend to your home for lunch. The dining
   room is decorated like a French cafe with candles and
   flowers. You're wearing a black skirt, white and black
   striped shirt with tights and a beret, and serve a salad
   nicoise and French baquettes, with Madelaines and French
   vanilla ice cream for dessert.

Which would be more personal to get as a gift from your significant other?

1. A shirt from Target.
2. A custom written poem on pretty stationary about your
   relationship in a picture frame.

What makes a nicer gift for Mother's Day?

1. A blouse from Ross.
2. A handmade collage with photos of you and your mom from over the years.

What sounds better?

1. At a store, you see a skirt you love that's twice as much as you can afford. The sales clerk asks, "Can I help you?" You say, "No, just looking," and walk away feeling sad you can't buy it.
2. At a store, you see a skirt you love that's twice as much as you can afford. You ask a salesgirl. "Do you know if this is going to go on sale anytime?" The salesgirl says, "Oh, this weekend everything in this department is 50 percent off." You ask her to hold it for you, and you buy it on Saturday.

You need a new toner cartridge for your printer, so you go to Staples. Which is smarter?

1. The toner cartridge is on sale for $49. You buy it.
2. The toner cartridge is on sale for $49. You check the same product on your smartphone. It comes up at Best Buy for $39 and at Amazon.com for $32. You tell the salesperson who looks it up. They charge you $32 for the toner.

A friend invites you to a concert in the park. What sounds better?

1. You politely decline, saying you have to stay home to wash your hair and pay bills. Your hair gets clean and you get aggravated with all your bills.

2. You go with your friend. You have fun. Meet a cool guy. He asks you out, and you start dating. He takes you to Hawaii and proposes. You get married and live happily ever after.

It's your spouse's or significant other's birthday. Which would he enjoy more?

1. A sweater from Nordstrom.
2. A four-bag-birthday, where you give him a choice. Bag # 1 has a negligee in it. Bag # 2 has a black mini-skirt, fish-net stockings and a long-stemmed rose. Bag # 3 has knee socks and a lollipop. Bag # 4 has a bustier and garters. You tell him to pick a bag for what he wants you to wear, with nothing else on. He picks all four bags. You oblige and have a hot sexy night!

Btw - If you choose a) – you need to improve your sex life! And FYI, I've done this!

13. How to Really *Become* a Millionaire

Okay, so if I knew how to do this, I wouldn't have written this book. But many others have authored books that tell you how. David Bach wrote a whole series of them, including *The Automatic Millionaire, Smart Women Finish Rich,* and *Start Late, Finish Rich.* Robert Kiyosaki wrote *Rich Dad, Poor Dad.* Other popular reads are *The Intelligent Investor* by Benjamin Graham and *Think and Grow Rich* by Napoleon Hill. A search on Amazon.com for "How to Become a Millionaire" brings up a slew of books offering practical information and guidance on the subject. Saving your money and growing it can lead to millionaire status. However, if you're not savvy about the stock market yourself, it's wise to find a good financial advisor who you can trust.

Of course, of all the potential ways to acquire millions, including those in the aforementioned books, most will probably take a lonnnnng time. So, while you're working on it, you'll still want to use the tips in all my chapters. Nonetheless, I offer a brief list of some of the ways it's possible to become a millionaire . . . perhaps, but not necessarily, in a relatively short time.

Inherit $$$

> "I made my money the old-fashioned way. I was very nice to a wealthy relative right before he died" – Malcolm Forbes

If you're lucky enough to be born into a family that has millions, my first sage tip is that you try not to alienate them. I have a friend whose father was a multimillionaire. The problem is that Jeff was a problem child, even as an adult, and his dad disinherited him. Poor Jeff. In more than one way!

If your family doesn't have a bundle, there are still ways to inherit a fortune. Make friends with rich people, and they might put you in their will. When I lived in New York, I had a wonderful hair stylist, Kyle, who used to do my hair for almost nothing, because he loved my thick tresses to practice on. (Did I mention, he was a great guy?) However, I went to the salon one day and he no longer worked there. His boss refused to tell me what happened or to what salon he'd moved.

A few years later I ran into Kyle at a party, and he told me the story. One of his previous clients was a cantankerous old widow who complained a lot. Still, when the old woman couldn't make it to the salon anymore, Kyle felt bad for her, so he'd go to her house, cut and color her hair, and then stay for dinner to keep her company. It wasn't always pleasant, since the elderly widow was often irritable and bitchy, kvetching about her life. He'd try to perk her up by taking her out to dinner sometimes and even to movies and shows. She'd always thank him, yet, regrettably, her mood never seemed to change.

But guess what! When the old woman died, she left two beautiful homes to Kyle along with a sizable amount of money. (Seems the woman's life wasn't so bad after all.) The funny thing is, Kyle was always broke before. He sold the two houses, bought a condo for himself, and put the rest of the proceeds into investment accounts or savings. He also quit his job and stopped doing hair . . . because suddenly he was a millionaire! A couple of years later, he moved to

Connecticut and opened his own salon. I thought this was a terrific story, not because he attained wealth, but because he was a talented nice guy, who truly cared about people.

As I indicated previously, it's always worthwhile to make new friends. And if you can be of service to someone who's old or ill, do a good deed. It may not pay you back in cash, but it will reap rewards in other ways. Give of yourself generously to all around you. You might be surprised. Someone you helped along the way may have been a secret millionaire . . . and you might be blessed with a bequest you never guessed!

You also might want to learn if you had rich relatives you never knew were rich! Check the unclaimed property sites mentioned in "The Whole Enchilada and Other Assorted Tidbits" chapter to see if any of your ancestors have money there. You never know – if they had funds from decades or centuries ago, it could have grown with interest . . . into millions.

Win the Lottery

We all know the things you need for this. Number One: You have to play to win. Number Two: You have to be lucky. So I can't recommend this as something you can really work toward or plan. The truth is, I've read about lots of lottery winners who cashed in . . . and then lost it all. I recently met a woman who told me her ex-husband won the state lottery. He immediately went out and bought a mansion as well as a dozen classic cars. He also headed to Las Vegas and made humongous bets with his new-found wealth. Suffice it to say, he started drinking, kept gambling and spending – and ended up with nothing. Including his wife, who left him!

Years ago, I saw a TV special on "Happiness" that pointed out that quadriplegics were *happier* than lottery winners. You know that old saying, "Money doesn't buy happiness." This TV show interviewed both rich and poor folks to show it was true. Duh. I don't know if I believe it, but it doesn't matter, does it? If you win the lottery, enjoy it, but try to put some of it away for more than a rainy day. And get yourself a good investment advisor . . . who's not named Madoff.

> **"I've done the calculation and your chances of winning the lottery are identical whether you play or not."** — Fran Lebowitz

Become an Entrepreneur

This actually makes the most sense, but it also means you must have the drive and the passion to do something. Most entrepreneurs spend years creating a business that ultimately makes them millionaires; it doesn't generally happen overnight. However, stories abound about those who have hit it big. People have become millionaires by inventing products, such as the hula hoop, Beanie Babies, or the Pet Rock. Baking cookies is what made Mrs. Fields rich and famous. And we all know about Mark Zuckerberg and Facebook. Did someone say "billionaire?"

In line with this, the Internet has made many millionaires. If you're savvy about how to become an affiliate, you can actually make tons of money without having a product or service yourself. Some people are tapping into multiple streams of income available from the web – and one way to do this is to become an "affiliate" for other sites and send people to buy those sites' products or services. It's a way to make money even while you sleep – but again, it takes work . . . and you have to know how to do it. Alas, why wasn't I born smart instead of adorable?!

Real Estate and Other Investments

"Don't buy shoes, buy buildings." –Nely Galen

We've always heard that it takes money to make money. And this is mostly true. Of course, once in a while, you'll hear, "No money down" and things like that. This really goes with being an entrepreneur. The secret is to buy something at a bargain price . . . then resell it, maybe after fixing it up . . . at a much higher price. Then repeat. Fix up. And repeat. Do it over and over, and you'll have millions in real estate. Sounds easy enough, huh? But you need to have the knowledge, smarts and ambition to do it.

From Rags-to-Riches . . . for Real!

Sometimes, having a skill can make you rich without your even knowing it. Especially if a little luck is in the mix. I heard the story of a young artist who painted a mural on a new company's wall. When he was done painting, the president of the company offered him a choice: The company could pay the artist for his work, then and there, or they could give him stock in the company. The artist didn't need the money at the time, so he agreed to take the stock. He went away, never expecting to see any money for his work. As it turns out, the company was a little startup called Facebook. And when they moved their original offices, they actually took along with them the wall with the young painter's mural. *Cut to:* Facebook becomes a multimillion-dollar company, and the young artist's shares are suddenly worth MILLIONS! Not bad for painting a mural! The young man was graffiti artist, David Choe. He painted the mural in 2005 when he had just gotten out of prison and was homeless. In 2012, when Facebook went public, his stock was worth $200 million!

Get on a Reality Show

Becoming famous can help you become a millionaire, even if you don't have any talent. The Kardashians are famous for this. They have built a zillion-dollar empire, and people still talk about the fact they have no actual talent. Then there are people like Snooki and *The Situation*, who became famous on the MTV reality show *Jersey Shore* and then started doing endorsements and creating their own brands. The thing they *did* have was a willingness to try out for a show, and to be publicly trashy and brashy . . . and it worked for them. A lot of reality shows have spawned "regular people" into stars . . . who then went on to become rich. Some had talent; some didn't. But fame begets money; the secret is to know how to handle it and keep it.

Then there's my favorite reality show, one that combines "becoming an entrepreneur" with "getting on a reality show" – *Shark Tank*. We can see right in front of us the creativity, inventiveness, and stick-to-itiveness these entrepreneurs all exude. They have passion, ambition, and a neverending belief in their product. And they WORK at it. So if you have a great idea and an entrepreneurial spirit, and enough energy to never give up, I say: *Go for it.*

Get on a Game Show

If you're smart, talented or adventurous, there are numerous game shows where contestants can win up to a million dollars: *Jeopardy* and *Who Wants to Be a Millionaire?* for brainiacs or trivia experts; *The Voice* and *America's Got Talent* for creative types; and for those who are physically fearless and forceful: *Survivor, American Ninja Warrior*, and the Netflix show, *Ultimate Beastmaster*. Even if you don't win a million, it's still fun, and you can walk away with enough to buy something, start a career, take a trip, whatever. In the chapter,

"That's Entertainment," I mention various ways to get into the audiences of game shows.

Become a YouTube, Snapchat, or Instagram Star

The Internet has opened up opportunities for all kinds of moneymaking schemes, scams and genuine businesses. Besides that, it's created an outlet for lots of creative and industrious self-starters who want to be in show business . . . but don't want to go through the rigors of the Hollywood system. YouTube, Snapchat, and Instagram are all examples of platforms where individuals have created their own shows or channels . . . and by getting millions of followers, they've now got millions of dollars. Maybe they didn't even do it to get rich; they started their channel because they had something to say – whether it be about fashion, makeup, games, or just acting weird or silly. Some of these people are Pewtie Pie, Jenna Marbles, Sara Hart, Glozelle Green, and many others. Of course, for every one that has become a millionaire – there are thousands or millions who haven't made poo. These Internet stars all have different stories, but they also have some things in common: they work at it; they're tenacious; and they keep at it.

The money may come to them in different ways. Sometimes, it's their partnerships or ads on the channel; sometimes, companies will sponsor them, i.e. give them money for their products to be featured on the show. Other times, it may be that their show has brought them to the attention of TV or movie producers who will hire them, or to commercial companies who will pay them to make videos. Sometimes, a popular YouTube celeb is paid $20,000 by an advertiser just to send out one tweet! The fact that they have millions of followers attracts big companies who want to do business with them. Some have been offered parts on TV shows or movies, but have declined, since they make enough money just sitting in their own living room, creating the videos they want – without having to answer to anyone else.

Check out some of their shows. They may seem simple, or they may not – but somehow, some way, these folks have caught the brass ring. Some have even given it back, finding that fame and fortune wasn't bringing them – oh no, there's that word again – happiness. But still, it's nice to know that in this contemporary world, you don't necessarily have to wait for Hollywood to call to bring your talent or message to the world – or to start bringing you the bucks.

Marry a Millionaire

Of course, you could always marry a millionaire. After reading this book, you'll be going where they go and living like one . . . so maybe you'll meet one and hit it off. Just remember, I get first dibs on any guy who looks like George Clooney!

I've had my chances with rich guys and, no question, I'd rather be with someone rich than with someone poor – but I'm not signing up for life with a guy just because he's wealthy. In fact, I could never marry a man if I didn't really love him. What's more, I need to be intellectually stimulated by him. My motto is "If I don't like him upstairs, I don't want to go downstairs!"

Write a Book

Just so you know, most authors don't make enough money from their books to support themselves. Most have "day jobs" and write because they love it or they are compelled to write a story or get a message out. But there are some who get lucky (there's that "luck" word again), and strike a chord with a massive audience. J.K. Rowling was turned down by tons of publishers before one finally said "yes" to *Harry Potter*. We know the rest of her story. She's now one of the richest women in the world. Jack Canfield's *Chicken Soup for the Soul* was another story of a book getting turned down by hundreds of places. Both of them became mega-hits with mega-sequels. And, of course, the *Harry Potter* books led to a whole series of blockbuster movies. Another example is *Fifty Shades of Grey;* it was a blog before it became the book that made E.L. James a millionaire. These authors believed in their work and pursued it without worrying about the rejections that they got over and over. They kept going. Okay, so now I'm hoping my book will somehow become a popular favorite, too. I could live with that.

Bottom line: it would be great if we could all become millionaires . . . but if we don't or even if we do . . . the ideas in this book can still be beneficial and fun, and help you keep those millions, too.

Chap Wrap 'n Recap

- Learn from Books
- Inherit $$$
- Win the Lottery
- Become an Entrepreneur or Real Estate Mogul
- Get on a Reality Show or Game Show
- Become a YouTube Star
- Marry Mr. or Mrs. Millionaire
- Write a Book

How to Become a Millionaire Quiz – True or False

It's easy to suddenly get zillions of dollars in your bank account if you....

1. Go on Shark Tank and pitch a time travel machine you invented that really works
2. Blast an email to seven hundred friends saying you're stranded in Nigeria, your wallet and passport were stolen, and you need $5,000 to be wired to you to get out of the country
3. Create a new app that every millennial must have, and charge $4.99 for the download
4. Make calls to a thousand strangers saying you're from the IRS and they owe $3,746 to be sent to your P.O. Box asap, or they will face charges and prison
5. Have millions of people buy your book, *How to Live Like a MILLIONAIRE When You're a Million Short!*

14. How to *FEEL* Like a Millionaire

"Content makes poor men rich; discontent makes rich men poor." –Benjamin Franklin

Finally, if you're reading this book, chances are you're not a millionaire. If you're not one – or even if you are – I would love it if this book has benefited you, and given you joy. And that, no matter how much money you have in the bank, you *feel* like a millionaire in your heart.

People can have all the money in the world and not be happy . . . or they can be broke as a skunk and be happy as clams. (Although I really don't know how happy a clam can be. I guess it depends if it's sitting in the ocean or steaming in a pot. It's probably not too happy steaming in a pot; although that makes *me* happy, since I'm probably about to eat it with spaghetti.)

In any case, I offer a few last words to help you to feel like a millionaire:

- Treat yourself well.
- Do things you like.
- Appreciate what you have.
- Don't sweat the small stuff.
- Laugh every day.
- Smile at people.
- Forgive.

- Give to others.
- Don't obsess over what you can't change.
- Most of all – enjoy life and all it has to offer.

Epilogue – Walking the Talk

Now that I'm finished writing my book, I think I deserve a little vacation. So I just called a bed and breakfast in Santa Barbara that normally charges $500 a night. I booked a room for two nights. No, it won't cost me $1,000. When I called the B&B, I asked to speak to the owner. I told him I'd write an article, and he agreed to host me for two complimentary nights. Plus, they serve a gourmet breakfast and have a happy hour every afternoon with wine and appetizers.

Of course, I want to look good on my trip, so the day before I leave, I want to get my hair done. I checked online at **www.SalonApprentice.com** and **www.Craigslist.com** under the beauty category, to see where they might need hair models. I found a hair stylist offering free blow outs and set up an appointment.

There are wonderful restaurants in Santa Barbara, so I logged on to **www.Restaurant.com** and redeemed a certificate for a cozy Italian bistro the first night. Then I went to **www.Groupon.com**. There was a sale for an extra 20 percent off their regular discounts, so I picked out a neat shellfish eatery for the second night and bought a Groupon for a super seafood meal at less than half the regular price!

Santa Barbara will be having First Thursdays when we arrive. It's a night of free art openings and music that is sure to be fun: **www.downtownsb.org/events/1st-thursday**. And during the day, I'll look for vintage shops in the area to see if they have any bargains. Also on my go-to list: several local wineries for their free tastings. Woo-hoo!

As any woman knows, I'll be going nuts packing for my mini-vacay. *What am I going to wear?* Hmmm, I'll check out **www.RentTheRunway.com** or **www.LeTote.com** and maybe rent some cool outfits for my hot getaway. Oh, and in the morning before leaving, I just might go to a department store cosmetic counter and get my make-up done for free – gotta look awesome on my travels!

My friend's birthday is that weekend and I need to get him a present. Since it's the beginning of the year, I bought him a wall calendar and I'm putting fun photos of us in different places throughout each month, along with funny sayings and stickers. Now, every time he turns a page, he'll see my personal paste-ups and get some smiles and laughs.

I'm coming back from my trip on Saturday night, and I've already gotten free tickets for what sounds like a fascinating play from **www.Soldoutcrowd.com**.

It should be a fantastic few days, without emptying my bank account!

Please let me know if *you've* done anything fun and fabulous, whether it's something you've learned about from reading this book, or something you've discovered on your own.

Here's how to reach me:

Website: **www.HowtoLiveLikeaMillionaire.com**

Facebook: **www.Facebook.com/howtolivelikeamillionaire**

Email: **www.HowtoLiveLikeaMillionaire@gmail.com.**

In the meantime, I'm wishing you lots of wonderful places to go and exciting things to do, and hoping you can live like a millionaire . . . even if you're a million short . . . like me.

XOXO,

Marilyn Anderson

Acknowledgements

This book has been a long time in the making and, from the first moment I envisioned it to finally getting it down on the computer, I've had lots of friends spur me on to write it and, more importantly, to finish it. Thanks to Wendy Kram, Fern Field, Catherine Clinch, and Michael Melamed for their constant enthusiasm and encouragement.

Over the years, I've told many friends and acquaintances my ideas and suggestions, and the book would not have happened without them. It's their willingness to use my advice and bargain tips, and tell me how well they worked, that led to my decision to write it all down.

Thanks to my dear friend, Marjorie Roseen, for being one of the first people to read a draft and tell me she loved it. Every writer should have a confidante like her to share late night phone calls with and discuss the emotional angst we go through in the process of getting our baby out to the world.

I want to thank my editor, Richard Crasta, for his wise input and feedback. And especially my writing partners on screenwriting projects, Richard Rossner and Dan Beckerman, who each acted as sounding boards whenever I needed another ear or eye, to run something by them or brainstorm over the phone.

My appreciation goes to John Seeley who shared his knowledge and experience on numerous things, including the bargains, discounts and living situations he has enjoyed over the years. Likewise, my gratitude goes to Stan Sinberg for adding some of his favorite money-saving ideas to the mix.

In this age of everything's-digital-and-electronic, I admit to being completely techno-challenged and appreciate the assistance I received from Danny Kastner on the Facebook page and Bill McGowan on website related matters. I'm also grateful to Jennifer Vally, Frank Chindamo, Mark Rappaport, David Gittins, and Janet Murphy who helped facilitate my Web Series for *How to Live Like a MILLIONAIRE When You're a Million Short.*

Special thanks to the authors and others who gave me pre-publication testimonial blurbs for the book: Chellie Campbell, BJ Gallagher, Wendy Kram, Felice Peres, Marc Fisher, Joel Eisenberg, Mark Miller, Catherine Clinch, Frank Chindamo, Karen Salkin, Rhonda Miller, Gerald Everett Jones, Jennifer Vally, Ellis Levinson, Bill Taub, and Michael J. Herman. I was thrilled that each of them offered to peruse the project, and I'm positively pleased with their praise.

I want to mention some other people who have been supportive and helpful along the way, including Christiana Miller, Roberta Edgar, and members of the organization, Independent Writers of Southern California.

Most of all, thanks to you, the readers, for whom I wrote this book. I hope you enjoy reading it and benefit from the information and my never-before revealed secrets.

About the Author

Marilyn Anderson is an award-winning television and film writer, author and playwright. She co-wrote and Executive Produced the 2015 family feature film, *How to Beat a Bully*. Marilyn has written for numerous television shows including *Murphy Brown, FAME, Sherman Oaks, Facts of Life, Friday the 13th – the Series,* and *Carol & Company*, starring Carol Burnett, Richard Kind and Jeremy Piven. She won a LUMINAS Award for the Positive Depiction of Women in Film and Television, and was honored by the Writers Guild of America as a writer of one of the 101 Best TV Shows of the past seven decades.

Ms. Anderson wrote and produced the Web Series, *How to Live Like a MILLIONAIRE When You're a Million Short*. She is also the host of the series, which complements the book.

In addition, Marilyn is the author of a humorous relationship book, *Never Kiss a Frog: A Girl's Guide to Creatures from the Dating Swamp*, published in ten countries. She also wrote and produced the *Never Kiss a Frog* Web Series, and co-authored the book, *MUTTweiler: An AutoDOGography*.

As a travel and entertainment reporter, Marilyn has written for various online magazines and in a column, *Romance on the Road*. Her witty relationship articles have appeared in the *Los Angeles Times* and other newspapers. She is also an accomplished speaker, and has been a guest on over 350 radio and TV shows, including *Extreme Makeover,* on which she was the Dating, Flirting and Kissing Coach.

Ms. Anderson currently lives in Los Angeles.

Visit Marilyn's Websites at:

- www.HowtoLiveLikeaMillionaire.com
- www.HowtoLiveLikeaMillionaire.info
- www.NeverKissaFrog.com
- www.HowtoBeataBullyTheMovie.com
- www.MarilynAndersonEntertainment.com

Your Ideas are Welcome!

If you have money-saving tips or suggestions you'd like to share, please send them to:

HowtoLiveLikeaMillionaire@gmail.com

Other Books by Marilyn Anderson

Never Kiss a Frog: A Girl's Guide to Creatures from the Dating Swamp

MUTTweiler: An AutoDOGography

Film by Marilyn Anderson

How to Beat a Bully

48978638R00162

Made in the USA
San Bernardino, CA
09 May 2017